Collector's Guide to
Burnt Wood Antiques

by

Frank L. Hahn

Copyright 1994   Golden Era Publications
ISBN # 0-926110-05-5

Assistance - Allan and Karen Nester
Color Photography - Keiko Hahn
Computer Work - Keiko Hahn

Published By
Golden Era Publications
A DIVISION OF GREEN GATE ENTERPRISES
P. O. Box 934
Lima, Ohio 45802

FOREWORD

It is hoped that the publication of this book will bring the art of pyrography to the attention of collectors. These pieces of folk art are approaching 100 years old, and have, in my estimation, been long overlooked and underpriced. Accordingly, unlike most other antiques, there are still a great many bargains to be found.

Frank L. Hahn

COVER PHOTO

1. Boy with Football Plaque. 9 7/8" x 13 1/2".
2. Indian Maiden Plaque. 6 3/4" x 11 1/4".
3. Round Lady's Head Plaque. Colored. Marked "Flemish Art #860". 12 1/2" x 17 1/4".
4. Palette Shaped Plaque. Carved. Marked "Flemish Art #374".
5. Girl with Cat Plaque. Carved. Marked "Flemish Art #860". 12 1/2" x 17 1/4".
6. Hinged Lid Box. A pyrography kit was contained in this box and the outside of the box had a design to be burned. Note the left side is not finished. 8 5/8" long x 6 1/8" deep x 5 1/8" high.
7. Scrap Basket. 14" high.
8. Small Hinged Lid Box with Woman's head. 6 1/4" long x 5 3/4" wide x 2 1/2" high.

COLOR PHOTO ON PAGE 3

9. Gibson Girl Plaque. 10 3/4" x 12".
10. Frame. Carved. 11" x 9".
11. Lady with Horse Plaque. Carved and Jeweled. Marked "Flemish Art #867". 9 7/8" x 14 7/8".
12. Horse's Head Plaque. Carved. Marked "Flemish Art #851". 7 5/8" diameter.
13. Lion's Head Plaque. Dated 1906 on back. 9 1/4" diameter.
14. Large Elk's Head Plaque in large burnt wood frame. Has "O. F. Proske" in large black letters on back. Also has "Mr. Otto F. Proske, 7 Lincoln St., Brunswick, Me." in smaller writing. Individually made and designed rather than a factory designed piece. 22 1/4" x 28 1/4".
15. Indian Maiden Plaque. Colored. Marked "Flemish Art #953". 8 7/8" x 20".

PYROGRAPHY

Pyrography is the art or process of producing a design or picture on wood, leather, cloth, etc., by burning or scorching the material used with a hot instrument. The word pyrography is not often heard, and more than a few dealers and collectors do not know its meaning, but mention burnt wood or Flemish Art, and most will immediately know what you are talking about.

The actual origin of pyrography is unknown, however, examples dating back to the 1400's have been found, and it is likely this art form was discovered well before that time. Pyrographic examples have been found all over Europe and the Orient, but, for the most part, the art form did not come to America until the mid 1800's, at which time skilled artists began to produce pieces here.

About 1890 articles on "burnt wood" began to appear in magazines, and by 1900 advertisements from companies supplying plaques, picture frames, bowls, compotes, steins, tie racks, boxes, and many other items, all with stamped designs on them for burning, were beginning to appear.

China painting, basketry, needlework and other forms of home arts and crafts were already popular in the United States, and the introduction of the stamped design on the raw materials made it possible for anyone, even those of limited artistic talent or ability, to participate in pyrography and create desirable and beautiful things. Accordingly, pyrography also became extremely popular.

Although wood burning is still being done today, the intended scope of this book is the period from 1890 to 1915 when it was most popular.

FLEMISH ART

The Flemish Art Company of New York was the largest producer of pyrography products. Their trademark was stamped on the back of many of the items they made, and that included hundreds of different shapes and thousands of different designs.

Since the products of other manufacturers were seldom marked with any identification, the term "Flemish Art" has become almost synonymous with burnt wood pieces of the early 1900's.

COLOR PHOTO ON PAGE 5

16.   Pedestal. Grape and Scroll Design. 30 1/2" high.

17.   Iris Design Stool. 12 1/8" top diameter. 14 7/8" high.

18.   Hinged Lid Dresser Box. 31 1/4" long x 5 1/4" Deep x 3 3/8" high. An example of a poorly burned piece. The burning is too shallow, and there is no contrasting color between the design and the background.

19.   Hinged Lid Box. Dated 1903. 15" long x 7 1/2" deep x 4" high.

20.   Hinged Lid Box. 14 3/4" long x 7 5/8" deep x 3 7/8" high.

21.   Woman's head and berries. An example of a Machine Scorched Hinged Lid Box. 9 1/2" long x 3 1/4" deep x 2 1/4" high.

22.   Monk Design Book Shaped Box with Sliding Drawer. Colored. 3 1/2" wide x 4 7'8" high x 1 1/4" thick.

23.   Pipe Smoker Design Book Shaped Box with Removable Lid. 3 3/4" wide x 4 1/4" high x 1 3/8" thick.

24.   Nine Sided Box with Removable Dome Lid. Has nine small burned panels which are held together by metal strips around the top and bottom edges. Has a metal bottom. 5" diameter x 2 1/8" high.

175
75
45
35
35
15
30
30
20

25. Dutch Girl. Colored. Marked "Flemish Art #859". 6 3/4" x 11 3/4".

26. Hunting Dogs Plaque. The art work and burning were both done by the pyrographer. Burned on the back is "From Hazel to Ora, Mary Christmas, 1907". Note that Merry is misspelled. 8 1/2" x 18".

27. Grapes Plaque. Colored. Marked "G. N. Co. #859". 6 3/4" x 11 3/4".

28. Picture Frame. 7 1/2" x 9 5/8".

29. Lion Plaque. On the back is "Made by B. Schmidt, 494 State St., B.K.L.Y.N." 19 3/4" diameter.

30. Oriental Lady Plaque. 5" x 11 3/8".

31. Fruit Basket Plaque. Color Tinted. 8" diameter.

32. Gibson Girl Plaque. On the back is "Compliments of Carrie Johnson, 1908". 7 7/8" x 9 3/4".

33. Hinged Lid Box. On the bottom in large black letters is "TOWER-MAJORS CANDY CO., The House of Chocolates, OTTUMWA, IOWA." Originally a candy box, the art work and burning were both done by the pyrographer. 14 5/8" long x 9 1/8" deep by 6 3/8" high.

34. Gibson Girl Hinged Lid Box. Very well done. Looks better than the photo as there are fine lines which do not show up well. 14 7/8" long x 7 5/8" deep x 4 1/4" high.

RESTORING BURNT WOOD PIECES

In searching for burnt wood pieces, it is not unusual to find pieces which are not in good condition. If inexpensive (some are priced as high as the nice ones), it is often worth the effort to restore them.

On pieces which have not had a finish applied, the wood may be dirty, and on pieces with a finish, the finish may have darkened with age, or have been too dark when originally applied. Dirty pieces may be cleaned with a sponge using Murphys Oil Soap and water, and fine steel wool may be used to further clean the wood.

Sometimes on pieces made with multi-layered wood, the glue has deteriorated and the layers are coming apart. A simple way to fix this is to spread the layers apart as far as is practical with a thin knife blade and force a good wood glue into the crack. Once this is done, spread cloth over the piece to protect the surface, put wood blocks over the cloth, if applicable, and clamp it together firmly with a wood clamp. Be sure to wipe off any excess glue that squirts out of the crack. Follows the instructions on the glue container and let the glue dry thoroughly before removing the wood clamp.

35. Book Shelf. 32 1/2" wide x 8 3/4" deep x 54 1/4" high.

Paint remover may be used, if necessary, to remove an old or discolored finish, and fine steel wool should then be used to further clean and smooth the surface. Murphy's Oil Soap and water is the best treatment for colored pieces as paint remover and steel wool may remove the color. The idea is to bring the piece back to a state where there is a nice contrast between the wood and the burning.

Once this is accomplished, the piece may be sprayed, if desired, with a satin finish polyurethane or shellac.   Should this result in a shinier finish than preferred, use steel wool to tone down the shine.

Practice makes perfect, and if you don't like the results, start over by removing the finish again, and reworking it until a more desirable appearance is achieved.

OTHER BURNT WOOD PRODUCTS

Some manufacturers of unrelated products, such as chocolates, gloves, etc., packaged their products in machine made containers with a design stamped or scorched onto the wood.

In some cases, a better skilled person with more artistic talent would often sketch out their own designs and apply them to wood. A point of further note is that, as pyrography became more popular, many of the craft pieces were made of laminated wood (usually three layers), so that the pieces could be carved as well as burned. Jewelled spangles of metal, metallic tinsel, glass jewels resembling precious stones, etc. were also available for further decorating.

OLD CATALOGS

Following the color pages are selected pages from a 1907 Flemish Art catalog. They have been enlarged to 8 1/2" x 11" from the original size of 7 1/2" x 9". Pyrographic products were sold by mail and by local businesses. This catalog was produced by the Flemish Art Company, and then imprinted with the name of a local Cortland, New York drug store which sold their products.

Selected pages from a Thayer & Chandler catalog follow the Flemish Art catalog.

By using catalogs of this type, far more pieces of pyrographic art material can be illustrated than would otherwise be possible. Since a number of manufacturers made products for burning, there are hundreds, if not thousands, of additional designs.

COLOR PHOTO ON PAGE 9

36.   Boy with Football Plaque. Marked "Flemish Art". 9 1/4" Diameter.

37.   Three Horses' Heads Plaque.   Carved.   Marked "Flemish Art #881"   14 5/8" x 20 1/2".

38.   Three Horses' Heads Small Plaque.   9 1/2" Diameter.

39.   Lady Plaque. 5 1/2" diameter.

40.   Boy Kissing a Girl Plaque. 5 7/8" diameter.

41.   "Their First Quarrel" Plaque. Signed " Edythe Jones" on front. 16 3/8" diameter.

42.   Dutch Girl Plaque. Carved. Marked "Flemish Art #856". 3 3/4" x 8".

43.   Indian Chief Plaque. Colored. Burnt on the back is "$9.75 - W.L.S." The price is undoubtedly what the pyrographer was asking for his creation. Looks better than the picture. 16" diameter.

44.   Hinged Book Rack. 15" long x 5 5/8" deep x 6 1/4" high.

45.   Foot Stool. Hinges and removable pegs make it collapsible. 14 1/8" long x 8" deep x 6" high.

46.   Dog's Head Hinged and Expandable Book Rack. Burnt on one side is "THERE IS NO PAST" and burnt on the other side is "SO LONG AS BOOKS SHALL LIVE". 15 5/8" long x 5 1/2" deep x 5 1/4" high. Expands to 25 1/2" long.

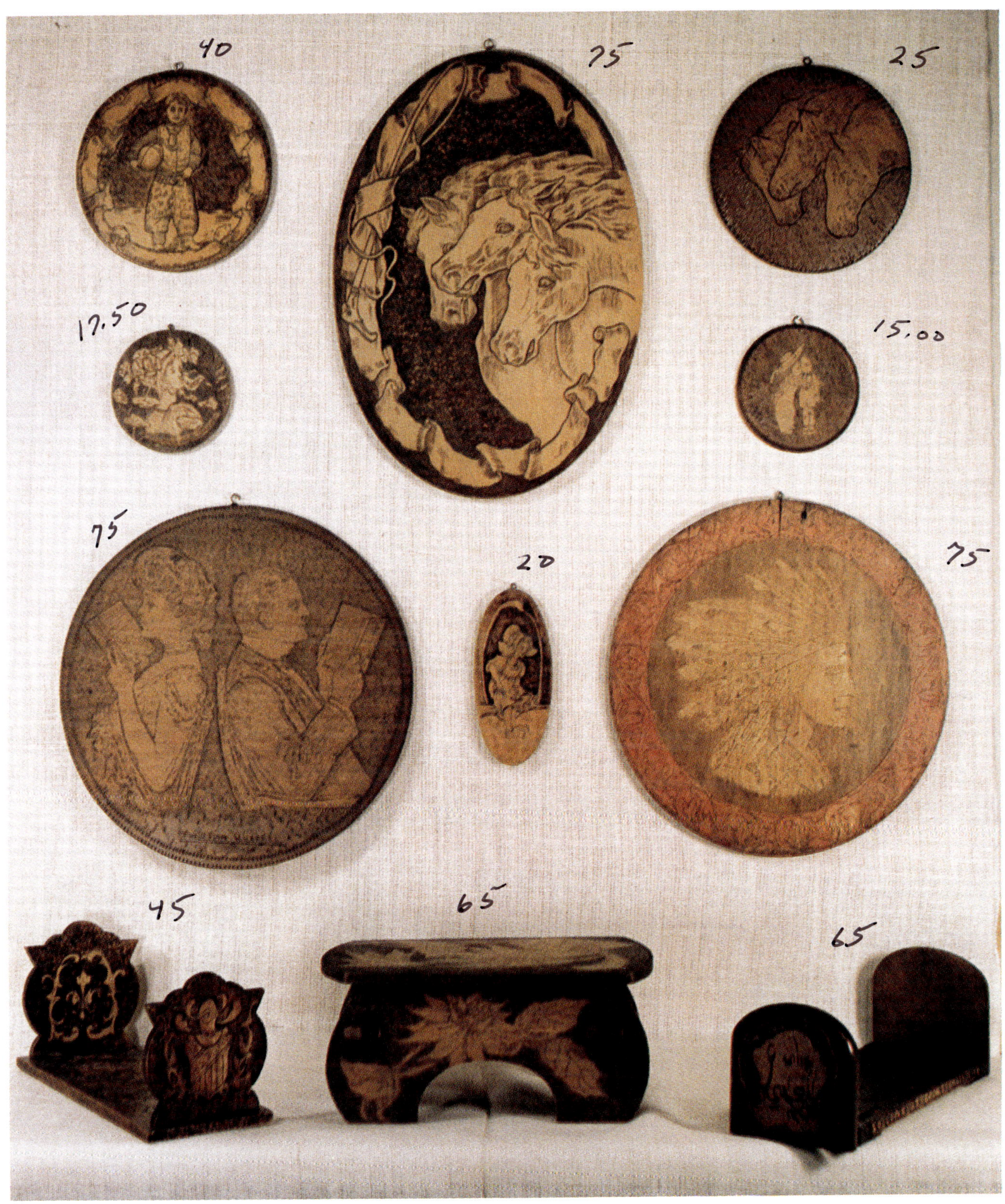

40
75
25
17,50
15.00
75
20
75
45
65
65

PRICES

Only a few years ago most pieces of pyrographic art were selling for under twenty five dollars, and numerous pieces could be purchased for five dollars or less. Many pieces are still available in the antiques market today, and the prices still seem comparatively low considering that they are a form of folk art. See the FOREWORD on page two.

In pricing pyrography it is important to differentiate between the three main types as follows:

(1) The machine-made stamped and scorched pieces, some of which were fairly attractive, but are not as nearly as desirable as the handcrafted ones. Once a few pieces have been examined, the stamped look, shallowness of design, and constant color become apparent.

(2) The pieces on which actual pyrographic burning has been done by an individual. This type is of interest to collectors, but in order to determine a value, consideration must be given to such qualities as (A) nicely or poorly burned, (B) the subject matter, (C) good or poor contrast, (D) overall condition, (E) is it jeweled, painted, carved, etc. Some of these qualities are often in the eye of the beholder, and only they are able to judge the desirability of a piece according to their own standards.

(3) The pieces on which the pyrographer had some artistic talent and did the art work in addition to burning it. In some cases, such as on pieces # 14 and # 26, the pyrographer also did the wood work and construction of the article to be burned. In the case of piece # 33, a candy box was used. Pieces of this type, if well done, are true pieces of folk art, and are accordingly the most desirable and valuable.

The prices in the price guide for this book are for pieces which are commonly judged to be in good condition, are nicely burned, and have good contrast.

OTHER MATERIALS

Materials such as leather, sheepskin, velvet, cloth, etc. were also used for burning, but are not included in this book since the burning of wood seems, by far, to have been the most popular. Also these materials were more subject to deterioration and to being discarded, so examples are relatively scarce.

COLOR PHOTO ON PAGE 11

47.   Lady with Flowing Hair Plaque. Jeweled.   7 3/4" x 18".

48.   Lady's Head Portrait Plate. Dated "1905". 9 3/4" diameter.

49.   Woman at Spinning Wheel Plaque. Written on the back is "Made by Mrs. Voight - 1909". 7 5/8" x 15 7/8".

50.   Oriental Lady with Fan Plaque. Marked "Flemish Art # 857". 4/3/4" x 10 1/2"

51.   Dog Plaque. Inscribed on the back is "Peter(?) Clingaman - Wauseon, Ohio - 1906 - Dover Center School". 5 3/4" diameter.

52.   Dutch Girl Plaque. 4 3/4" x 10 1/2".

53.   Roses in Vase Plaque. Carved. Marked "Flemish Art # 854". 14 3/4" diameter. Piece # 80 is another example of the same design plaque.

80.   Grapes Plaque. Colored. 13 5/8" diameter.

81.   Thermometer. 3 7/8" x 7 7/8".

82.   Woman with Fruit Basket Plaque. Carved. Inscribed "Xmas - 1910". Nicely done. 11 5/8" diameter.

83.   Framed Lady's Head Plaque. The construction, art work, and burning were all done by the pyrographer. 8 1/4" wide x 8" high.

84.   Woman with Crown Plaque. Colored. 15 5/8" x 19 3/4".

85.   Sunbonnet Babies "Wash Day" Plaque. Colored. Nicely done with desirable subject matter. 8" x 9 7/8".

86.   Roses in Vase Plaque. Carved. Marked "Flemish Art # 854". Signed on front "Elizabeth Osga--- - 1906" This is the same style plaque as piece # 53, but is more finely burnt, and illustrates the difference careful staining can make in appearence. 14 5/8" diameter.

87.   Woman's Head Plaque. Marked "Flemish Art # 862". Dated 2-7-1910. 5" x 11".

88.   Lady's Head Plaque. Well decorated with Jewels and Jewelry. On the back is "From George McMillen - Dec. 25/06. Wishing you a Merry Xmas". 15 3/4" diameter.

89. Indian Maiden with Jewels Plaque. Carved. Flemish Art #881. 12" x 18". On the back is "Clinton - Oct. 4 - 1900 - Knisely"
90. Fruit Plaque. Colored. 9 1/2" x 19 1/2".
91. Indian Brave with Jewels Plaque. Carved. Flemish Art #881.
92. Woman with Flowers Plaque. Colored. Flemish Art # 853. 11 3/4" diameter.

(16)

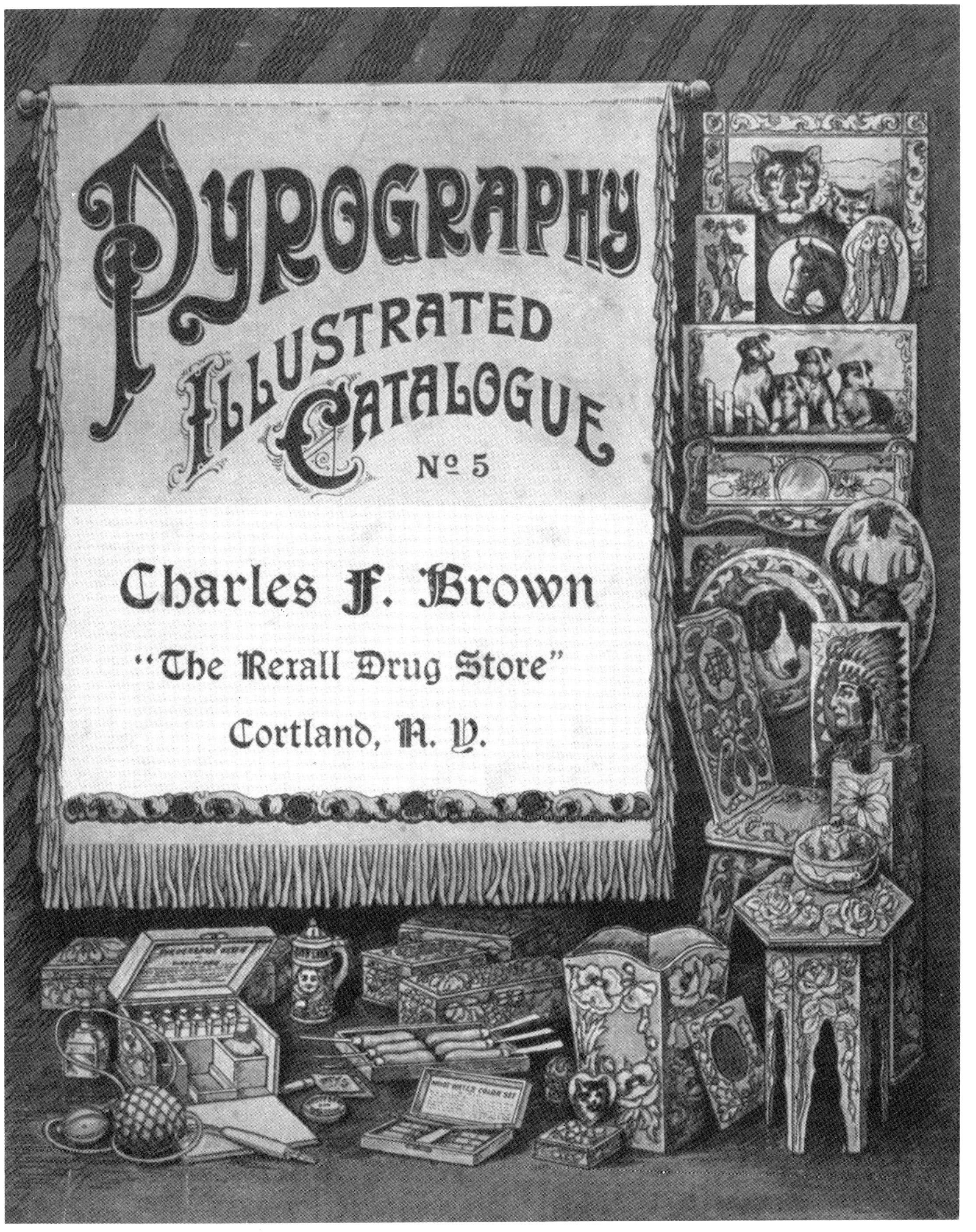

PYROGRAPHY
ILLUSTRATED
CATALOGUE
No 5
Charles F. Brown
"The Rexall Drug Store"
Cortland, N. Y.

CATALOGUE
No. 5

OF

BEAUTIFUL
FASCINATING
PYROGRAPHY

PRICES SUBJECT TO CHANGE
WITHOUT NOTICE

THE MOST COMPLETE CATALOGUE
OF PYROGRAPHIC NOVELTIES
AND SUPPLIES EVER
PUBLISHED

EVERY ARTICLE LISTED HEREIN IS MANUFACTURED BY THE LARGEST
AND BEST-KNOWN PYROGRAPHIC FACTORY IN THE WORLD,
AND GUARANTEED BY THEM

PYROGRAPHIC OUTFITS

No. BM OUTFIT

Represents a fine beginner's or school outfit; contains all necessary articles for doing work properly, and has given great satisfaction. The articles as enumerated are well packed in neatly designed basswood boxes shown. Price, **$2.00**.

Price with No. 58 Carving Knife and No. 61 Carving Chisel, **$2.50**.

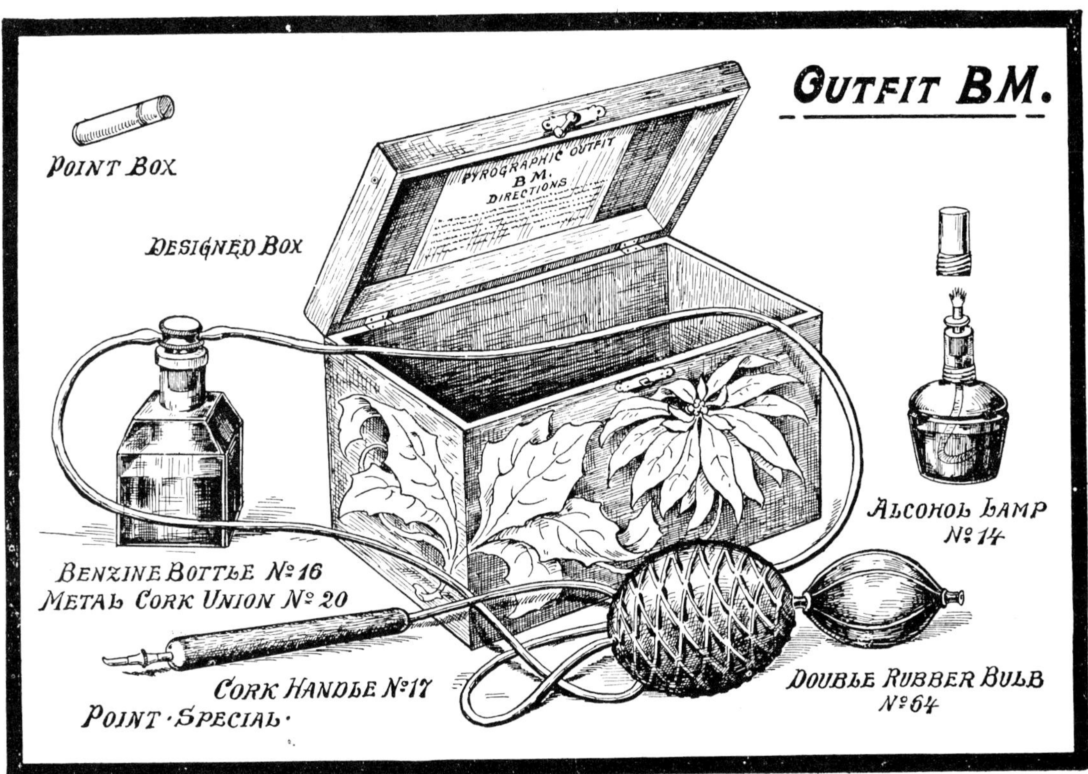

No. L OUTFIT

Much the same as our B M, with the added advantage of a better point, larger box, and the addition of several practice pieces to test points when beginning your work. A very popular, medium priced outfit that will give good service for average work. Price, **$2.50**

Price with No. 58 Carving Knife and No. 61 Carving Chisel, **$3.00**.

BE SURE TO FOLLOW DIRECTIONS CAREFULLY IN ORDER TO SECURE RESULTS

No. V OUTFIT

Combines all the new and excellent features of previous outfits with the addition of our patent swivel handle. Outfit is furnished in practical and convenient drop front flap designed basswood box, partitioned inside for benzine bottle, alcohol lamp, and one bottle each of stain and gloss. Price, each, **$4.00**.

Price with No. 58 Carving Knife and No. 61 Carving Chisel, **$4.50**.

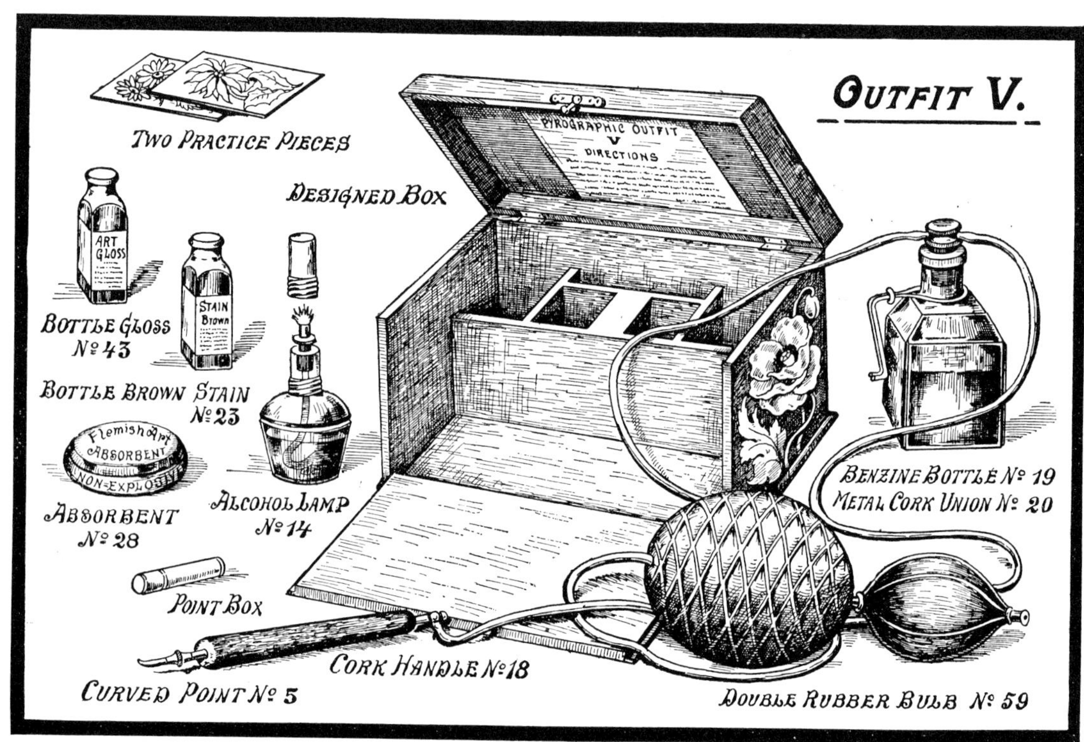

No. R OUTFIT

Very like the V listed above, but has the advantage of being fitted with one of the better grade (heavier) platinum points, such as used by professionals. This is one of the most popular of the better grade outfits, and thousands are now in use. Price, **$4.50**.

Price with No. 58 Carving Knife and No. 61 Carving Chisel, **$5.00**.

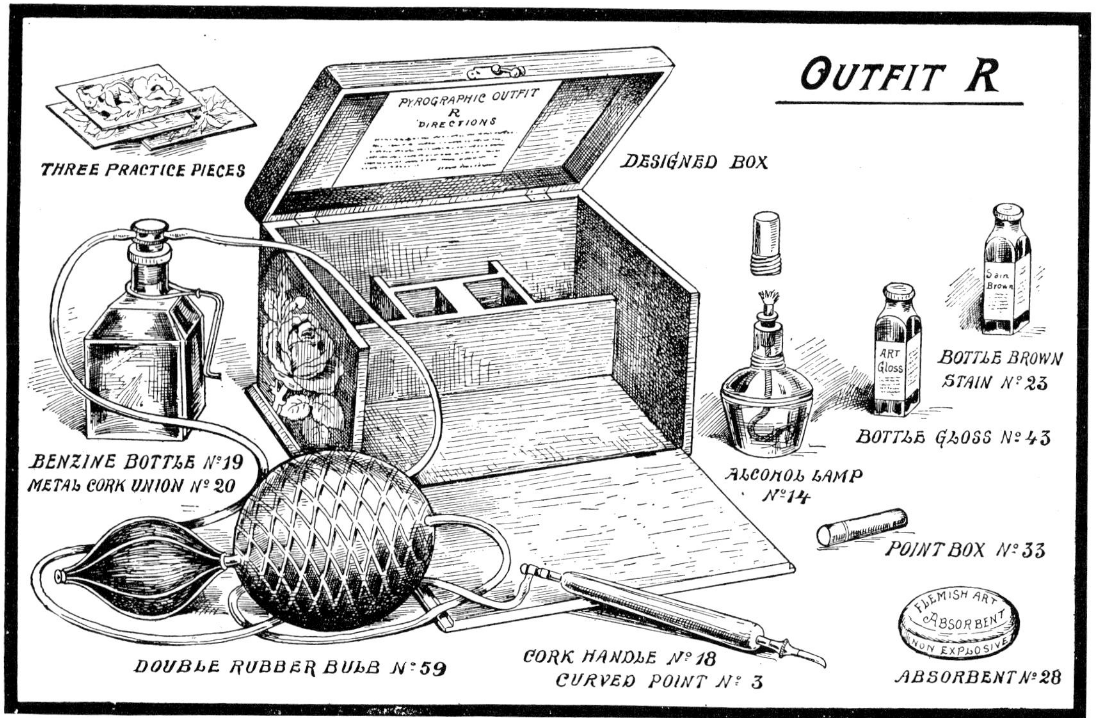

WE GUARANTEE ALL OUR POINTS AND OUTFITS TO BE PERFECT WHEN THEY LEAVE OUR ESTABLISHMENT

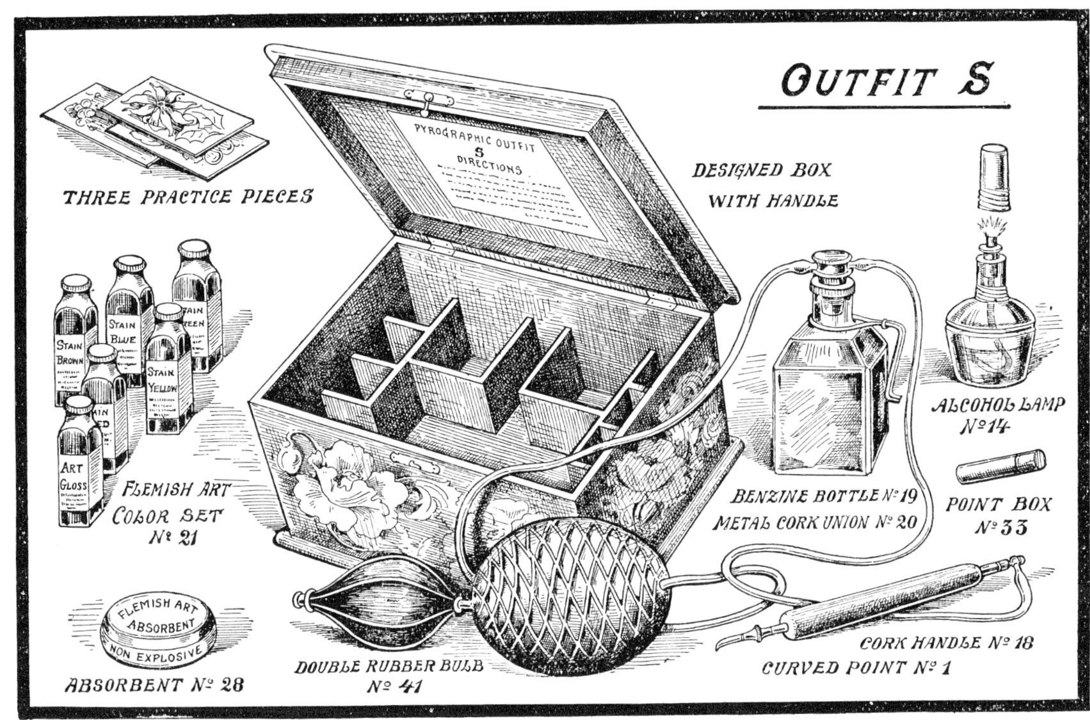

No. S OUTFIT

Represents the highest grade we can offer, is fitted with the best possible sundries, and can be relied upon to give perfect satisfaction for all around work. It is fitted with a very heavy point. (Our No. 1) has a complete staining and coloring outfit (5 assorted colors and 1 bottle art gloss); is packed in extra large partitioned selected white basswood box, elegantly designed; also has a large size double bulb. Box has brass handle for convenience in carrying. Price, **$5.00**.

Price with No. 58 Carving Knife and No. 61 Carving Chisel, **$5.50.**

No. T OUTFIT

Is adapted for **Foot Power,** which means that bulbs are operated by foot, leaving hands free; has No. 3 point, which is suitable for all styles of work, and all other fittings are of the very best grade. Price, $6.00.

Price with No. 58 Carving Knife and No. 61 Carving Chisel, $6.50.

NOTE THE NEW COLORS, ½ PANS AND TUBES. GIVE MOST SATISFACTION AND ALLOW PERFECT SHADING AND BLENDING

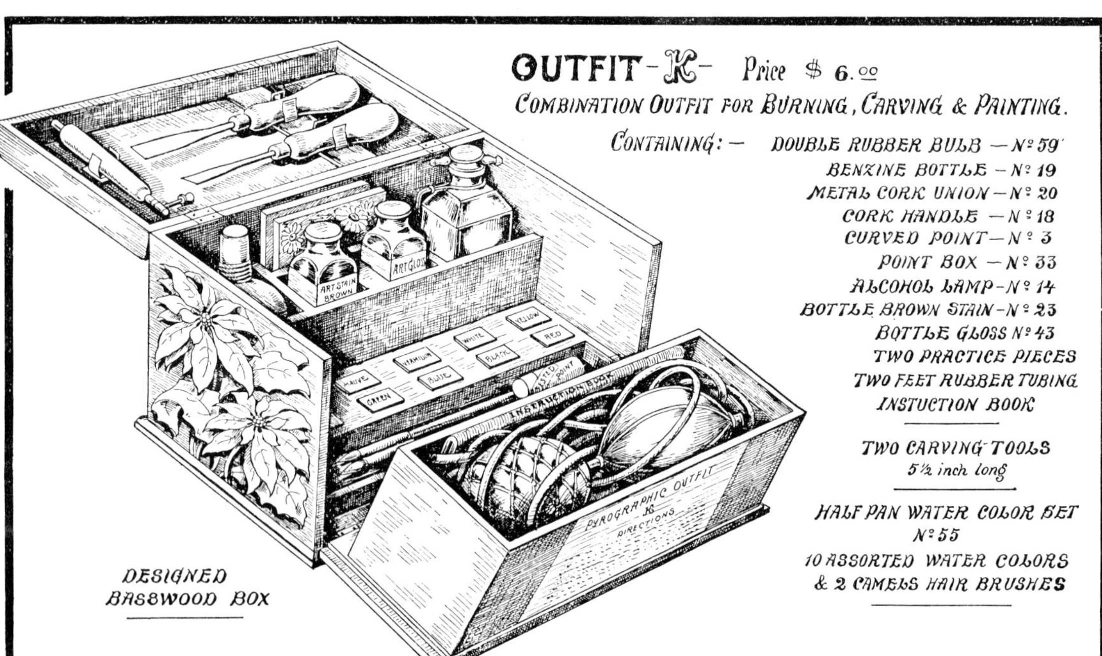

The COMBINATION OUTFITS

For burning, coloring and carving. Contain finest fittings and are splendid gift sets. Price, K Outfit, **$6.00,** including carving tools.

X OUTFITS

With six splendid steel tools for carving and six tubes imported water color paints, as shown, make a combination outfit unsurpassed as to quality and fittings. Price, **$7.50.**

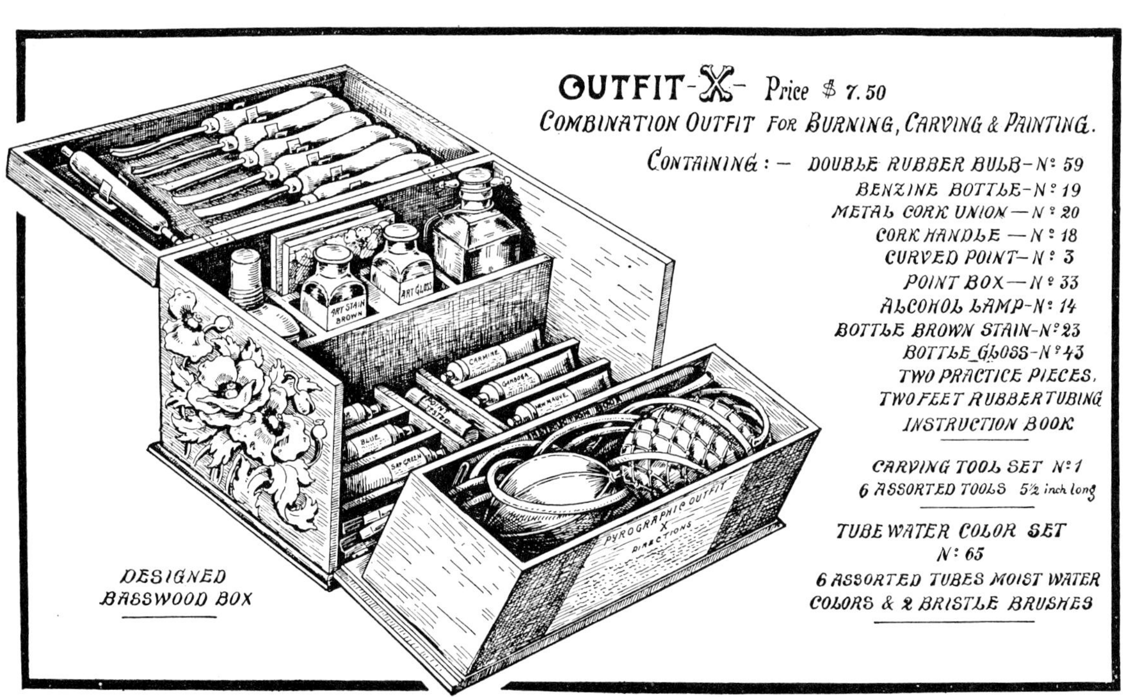

CARVING TOOLS FURNISHED WITH ALL OUR OUTFITS IF DESIRED AT A SLIGHT ADDITION IN PRICE AS SHOWN IN PREVIOUS PAGES

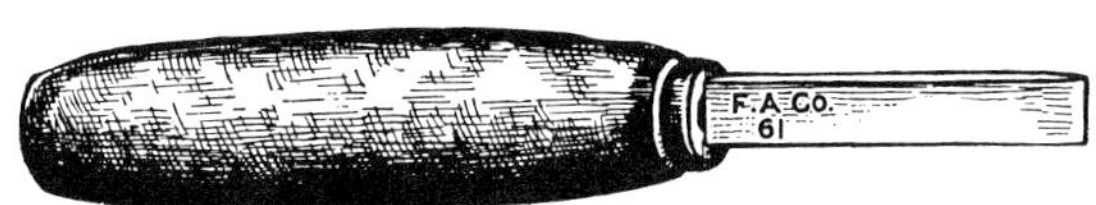

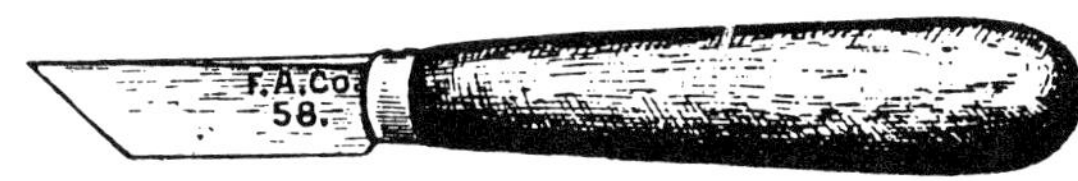

No. 61   CARVING CHISEL

Specially manufactured by us for use with No. 58 Knife, and is of finest quality steel with good edge, and is very easy to manipulate.

Price, each, . .	$0.30
Dozen, . . .	3.50

This is a knife of finest razor steel, hardened by the new electric process; has a perfect edge, and is very pliable and easily handled. We are manufacturing this knife for carving the 3-ply articles of our line.

Price, each, . .	$0.30
Dozen, . . .	3.50

JEWELLED SPANGLES
OF METAL

For decorating placques, etc., ALL COLORS. These are simply glued to article to be decorated, showing up necklaces, head-dresses, etc., beautifully. Also as dew on leaves, flowers, etc.

Price, per 1,000, 80c.

SPARKLING METALLIC TINSEL

A beautiful and effective substitute for beads and one that is very simple of application to Pyrographic wood, showing the most surpassingly beautiful results. When used in connection with jewels shown on opposite side of page, striking effects are obtained. Full directions with every vial. Colors furnished are:

Green	Blue	Red
Purple	Gold	Silver
	Copper	

Price per vial   .   30c.

ADHESIVE

Adhesive for tinsel, per bot. 25c.

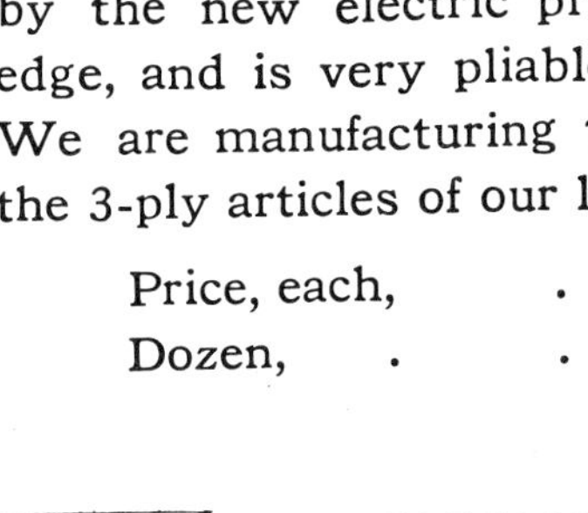

The most up-to-date, concise and complete work on pyrography published. Every process or little hint possible is given. Also has thirty half-tones of backgrounds, lines, etc.

Price, 15c. each.

BRILLIANT GLASS JEWELS

Add lustre and give a luxurious finish to pyrographic designs, such as beads, necklaces, belts. All styles, such as

Diamonds	Topaz
Rubies	Turquoise
Emeralds	Garnets
Sapphires	Opals
Coral	Amethysts
Etc.	

In all sizes.   Prices are per 100.

Size A
Price, 50c.

Size B
Price, 50c.

Size C
Price, 60c.

Size E
Price, $1.50

Size D
Price, $1.00

Size G
Price, $3.00

Size F
Price, $2.50

LEATHER FRINGE for cushions of selected Ooze Skins. All popular colors, such as red, brown, tan, green, etc., etc. Per package of 4 pieces, each 24 inches long. Enough for one cushion, complete.
2 inches wide, 90c. package.   3 inches wide, $1.20 package

LEATHER LACINGS for making leather post card pillows, etc. All popular colors. Price, per dozen pieces, each 36 inches in length, 60c.

THREE-PLY BASSWOOD PANELS

852 Des. D.B.   852 Des. F.H. No. 3.   852 Des. B.P.   852 Des. J.N.

852 Des. F.H.   852 Des. D.G   852 Des. P.H.   852 Des. E.K

Price $ 0.25 each, $ 2.50 p.doz.

866 Des. C.P. (7" X 16")   866 Des. D.G. (7" X 16")

866 Des. C.S.   866 Des. F.G.   866 Des. J.   866 Des. J.A.   866 Des. J.C.

Price $ 0.25 each $ 2.50 p.doz.

THREE-PLY BASSWOOD PANELS

859 Des. T.G.   859 Des. J.G.   859 Des. D.G.   859 Des. F.B.   859 Des. C.G.

(7" × 12")   Price $ 0.25 each $ 2.50 p. doz.   (7" × 12")

865 Des. R.G.   (9" × 12")   865 Des. G.S.   865 Des. F.B.   (9" × 12")   865 Des. A.H.

Price $ 0.25 each $ 2.50 p. doz.

938 Des. H.C. (6" × 18")

938 Des. C.P. (6" × 18")

Price $ 0.25 each $ 2.50 p. doz.

938 Des. M.D.   938 Des. D.G.

THRE-PLY BASSWOOD PANELS

853 Des. F.H. (12" diam.)
No. 12.

853 Des. F.H. (12" diam.)
No. 1.
Price $ 0.25 each $ 3.00 p. doz.

853 Des. I.G. (12" diam.)

853 Des. D.D. (12" diam.)

853 Des. F.H. (12" diam.)
No. 9.
Price $ 0.25 each $ 3.00 p. doz.

853 Des. J.M. (12" diam.)

853 Des. B.D. (12" diam.)

853 Des. J.N. (12" diam.)

853 Des. P.D. (12" diam.)

THREE PLY BASSWOOD PANELS

853 Des. L. N
(12" diam)

853 Des. E. K
(12" diam.)

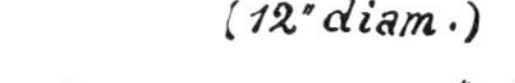

853 Des. T. R

Price $ 0.25 each $ 3.00 p. doz.

853 Des. H. L
(12" diam)

853 Des. P. H
(12" diam.)

853 Des. H. R
(12" diam)

Price $ 0.25 each $ 3.00 p. doz.

853 Des. B. D (12" diam.)

853 Des. H. D (12" diam.)

854 Des. G. D (12" diam.)

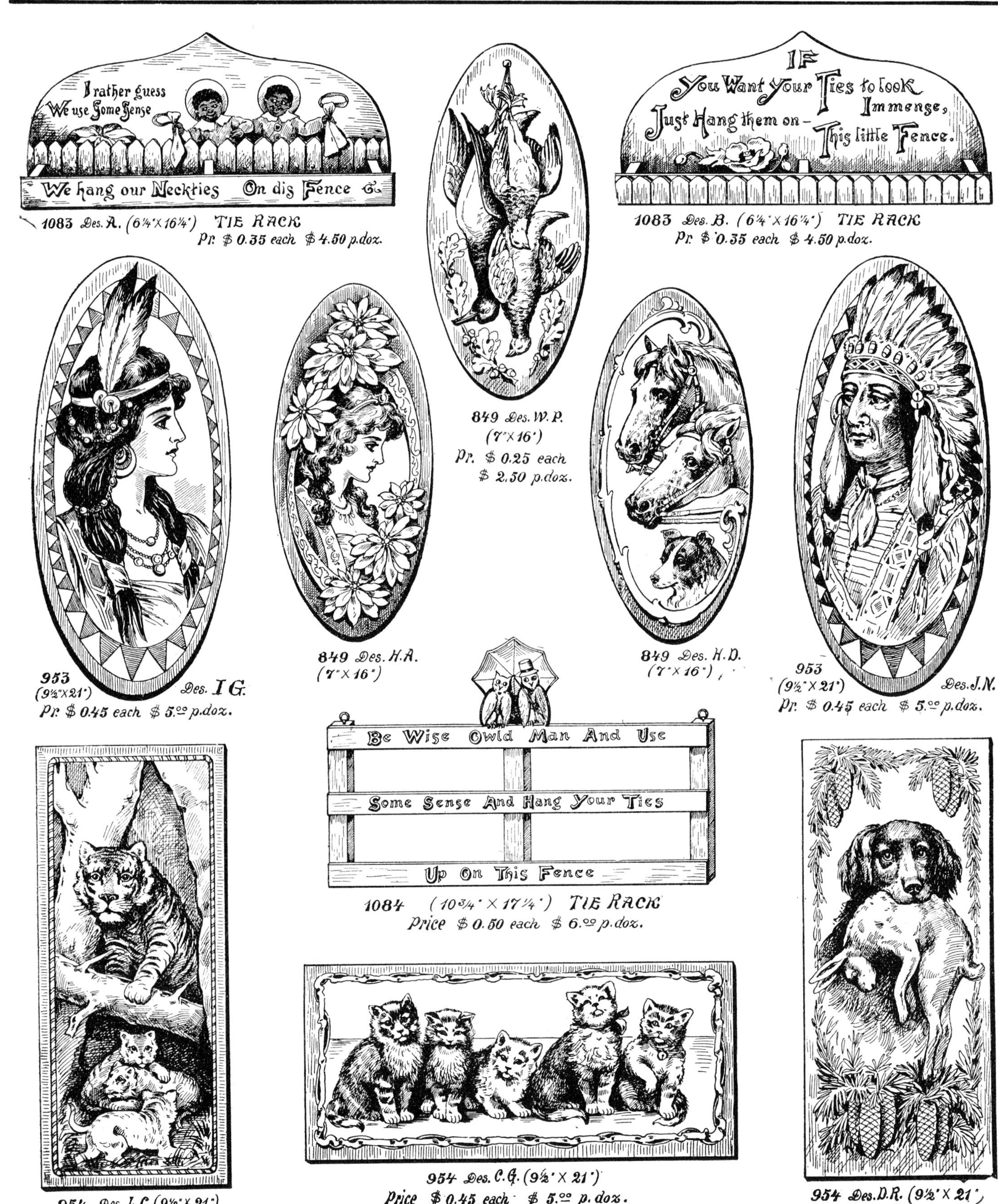

1083 Des. A. (6¼"×16¼")   TIE RACK
Pr. $ 0.35 each $ 4.50 p.doz.

1083 Des. B. (6¼"×16¼")   TIE RACK
Pr. $ 0.35 each $ 4.50 p.doz.

849 Des. W. P.
(7"×16")
Pr. $ 0.25 each
$ 2.50 p.doz.

953
(9½"×21")
Des. I G.
Pr. $ 0.45 each $ 5.00 p.doz.

849 Des. H. A.
(7"×16")

849 Des. H. D.
(7"×16")

953
(9½"×21")
Des. J. N.
Pr. $ 0.45 each $ 5.00 p.doz.

1084   (10¾"×17¼")   TIE RACK
Price $ 0.50 each $ 6.00 p.doz.

954 Des. L. C. (9½"×21")

954 Des. C. G. (9½"×21")
Price $ 0.45 each $ 5.00 p.doz.

954 Des. D. R. (9½"×21")

THREE PLY BASSWOOD PANELS

881 Des. F.H. (12" x 18")

881 Des. D.D. (12" x 18")

881 Des. F.G. (12" x 18")

881 Des. T.C. (12" x 18")

Price:
$ 0.45 each
$ 5.00 p.doz.

881 Des. H.M (12" x 18")

881 Des. T.R. (12" x 18")

881 Des. J.N. (12" x 18")

881 Des. P.H (12" x 18")

854 (15" diam) Des. K.O.P.

854 (15" diam) Des. I.O.O.F.

853 Des. B.L.
(12" diam.)

854 (15" diam) Des. E.S.

854 (15" diam) Des. F.o.A.

853 Des. K.T.
(12" diam.)
Price $0.25 each
$3.00 p. doz.

854 (15" diam) Des. K.o.C.
Price $0.45 each $5.00 p. doz.

854 (15" diam) Des. R.A.
Price $0.45 each $5.00 p. doz.

PLACQUE

PLACQUE

658 Des. T. E. (12" diam.)

658 Des. P. H. (12" diam.)
Price $ 0.70 each $ 8.00 p. doz.

658 Des. T. D. (12" diam.)

PLACQUE
Price $ 1.35 each $ 16.00 p. doz.

660 Des. D. C. (18" diam.)

660 Des. F. S. (18" diam.)

PLACQUE

PLACQUE

658 Des. F. S. (12" diam.)

658 Des. H. D. (12" diam.)
Price $ 0.70 each $ 8.00 p. doz.

658 Des. J. N. (12" diam.)

659 Des T. PLAQUE (15″diam.) Pr. $ 1.⁰⁰ each
$ 12.⁰⁰ p. doz.

659 Des. L.N. PLAQUE (15″diam.) Pr. $ 1.⁰⁰ each
$ 12.⁰⁰ p. doz.

659 Des.T.D. PLAQUE (15″diam.) Pr. $ 1.⁰⁰ each
$ 12.⁰⁰ p. doz.

662 Des. H.S. PLAQUE (24″diam.) Pr. $ 2.⁰⁰ each
$ 24.⁰⁰ p. doz.

662 Des. N.A.D. PLAQUE (24″diam.) Pr. $ 2.⁰⁰ each
$ 24.⁰⁰ p. doz.

1058   Des. L.N. (13"x 17")
CAGE FRAME Price $ 0.80 each
$ 9.60 p.doz.

1082 Des. B.C.
CAGE FRAME (10"x 13")
Price $ 0.50 each. $ 6.00 p.doz.

1058   Des. T.R. (13"x 17")
CAGE FRAME Price $ 0.80 each
$ 9.60 p.doz.

1059 Des. T.R. (16"x 20") CAGE FRAME Price $ 1.00 each
$ 12.00 p.doz.

1059 Des. L.N. (16"x 20") CAGE FRAME Price $ 1.00 each
$ 12.00 p.doz.

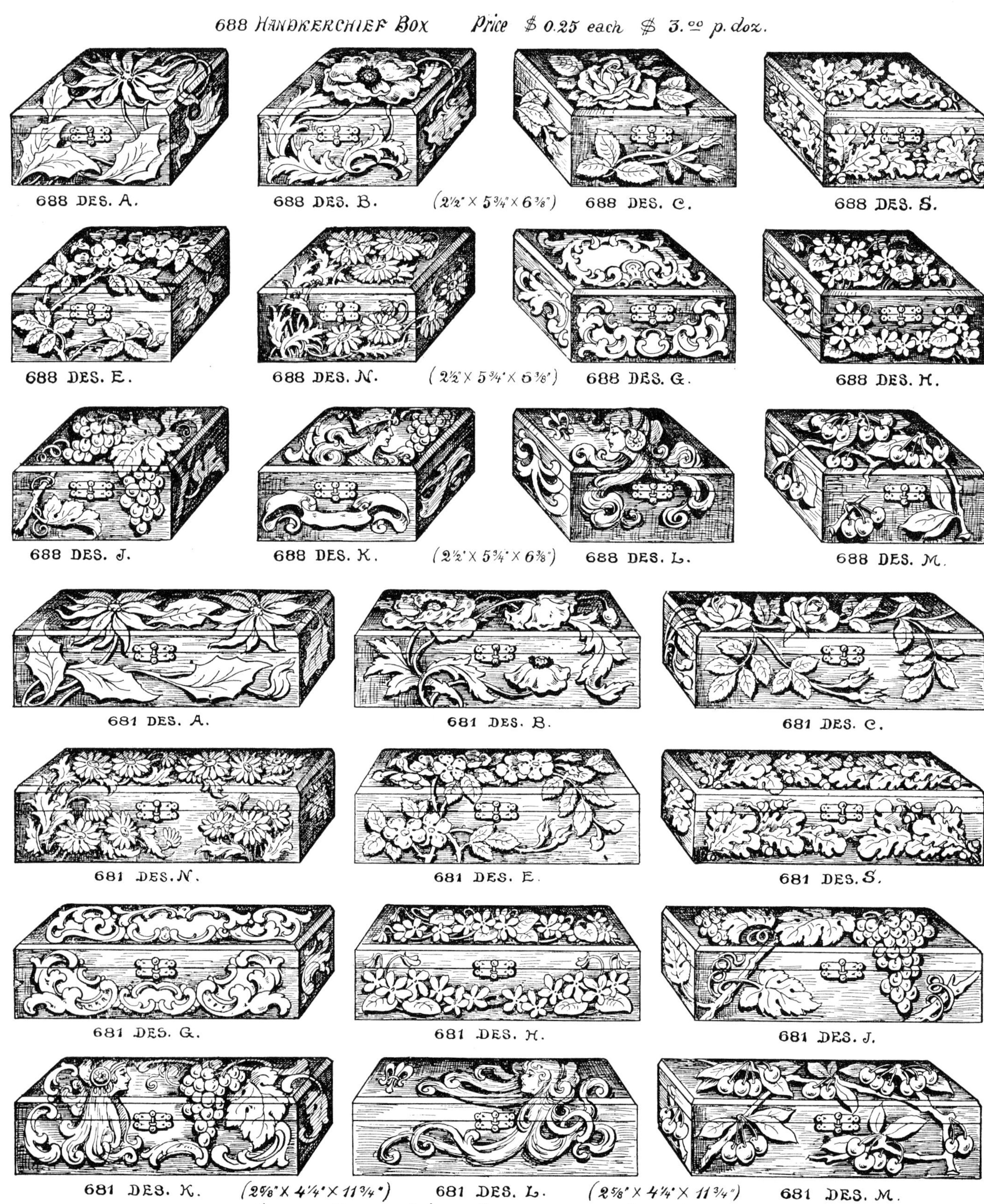
688 HANDKERCHIEF BOX   Price $ 0.25 each $ 3.00 p. doz.
688 DES. A.   688 DES. B.   (2½" × 5¾" × 6⅜")   688 DES. C.   688 DES. S.
688 DES. E.   688 DES. N.   (2½" × 5¾" × 6⅜")   688 DES. G.   688 DES. H.
688 DES. J.   688 DES. K.   (2½" × 5¾" × 6⅜")   688 DES. L.   688 DES. M.
681 DES. A.   681 DES. B.   681 DES. C.
681 DES. N.   681 DES. E.   681 DES. S.
681 DES. G.   681 DES. H.   681 DES. J.
681 DES. K.   (2⅝" × 4¼" × 11¾")   681 DES. L.   (2⅝" × 4¼" × 11¾")   681 DES. M.
GLOVE BOX   Price $ 0.25 each $ 3.00 p. doz.

695 Des. C
695 Des. D
695 Des. E
695 Des. F
695 Des. G
695 Des. H
695 Des. J
695 Des. L
695 Des. M
695 Des. N
JEWEL BOX   (2½" × 3½" × 4½") Price $0.21 each $2.50 p. doz.
685 Des. A
685 Des. B
685 Des. C
685 Des. S
685 Des. E
685 Des. Z
685 Des. G
685 Des. P
685 Des. J
685 Des. K
(5¼" × 6" × 6")
685 Des. U
685 Des. M
COLLAR AND CUFF BOX Price $0.35 each $4.00 p. doz.

778. Des. A.   (3½" × 5" × 31")
DRESSER BOX Price $ 1.45 each $ 17.00 p.doz.

692
Des. H. (2¾" × 3¼" × 4½")
JEWEL CHEST

778 Des. C.   (3½" × 5" × 31")
DRESSER BOX Price $ 1.45 each $ 17.00 p.doz.

692.
Des. N. (2¾" × 3¼" × 4½")
JEWEL CHEST

778. Des H.   (3½" × 5" × 31")
DRESSER BOX Price $ 1.45 each $ 17.00 p.doz.

692
Des. M. (2¾" × 3¼" × 4½")
JEWEL CHEST Pr. $ 0.35 each
$ 4.00 p.doz.

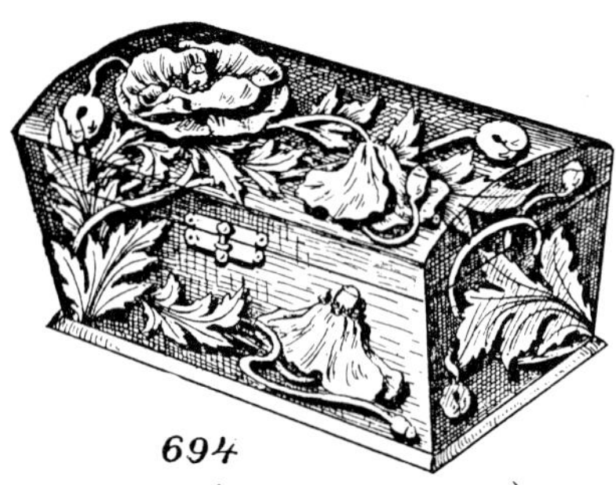

694
Des. B. (3½" × 4¼" × 7¾")
JEWEL CHEST

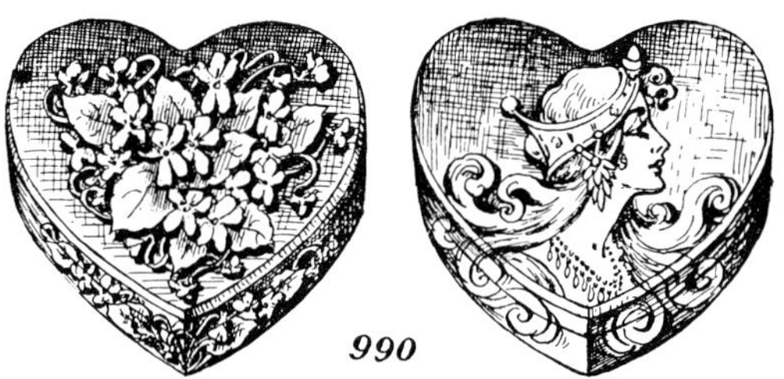

990

Des. H.   (2⅛" × 5⅞" × 6¼")   Des. L.
JEWEL BOX Price $ 0.70 each
" 8.00 p.doz.

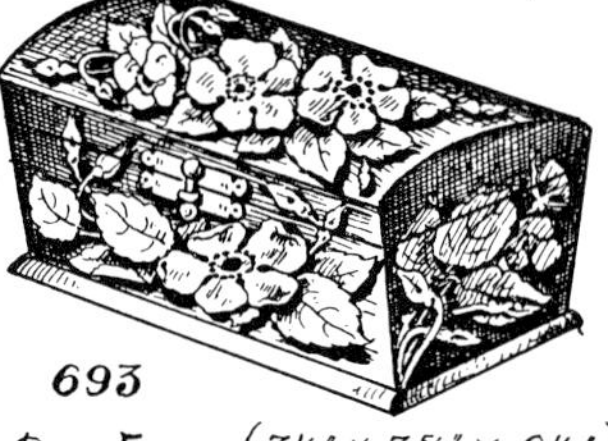

693
Des. E.   (3½" × 3⅝" × 6¼")
JEWEL CHEST

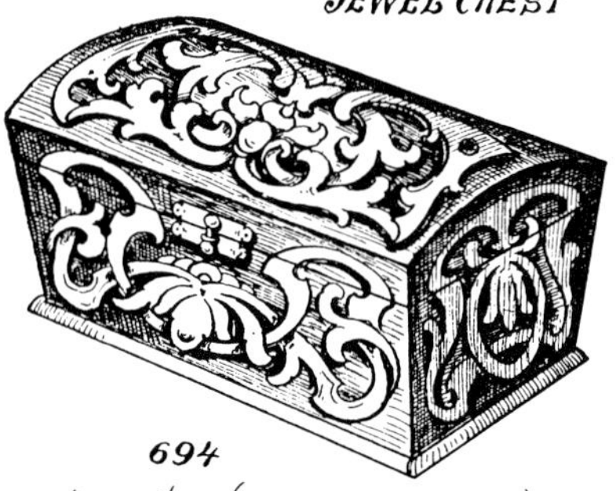

694
Des. G. (3½" × 4¼" × 7¾")
JEWEL CHEST   Pr. $ 0.50 each
6.00 p.doz.

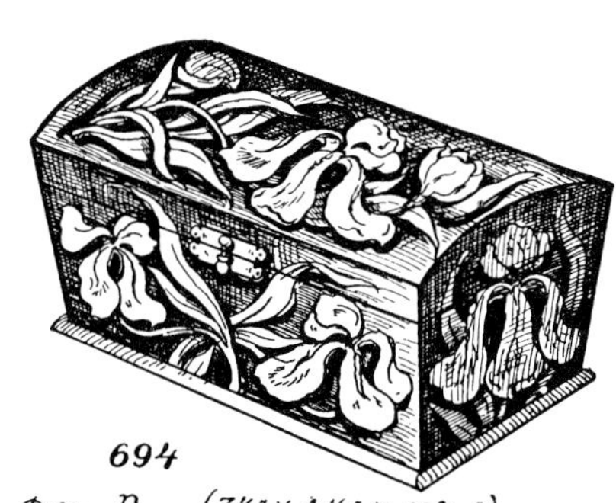

694
Des. P.   (3½" × 4¼" × 7¾")
JEWEL CHEST

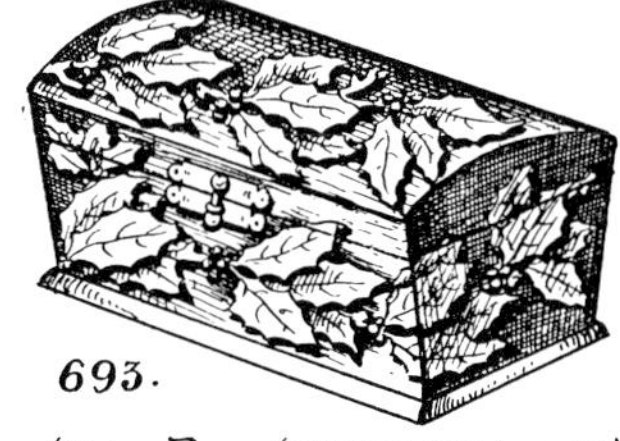

693.
Des. F.   (3½" × 3⅝" × 6¼")
JEWEL CHEST

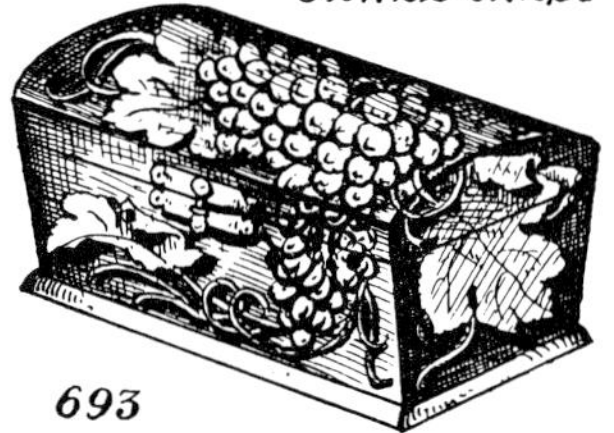

693
Des. J.   (3½" × 3⅝" × 6¼")
JEWEL CHEST Pr. $ 0.45 each
5.00 p.doz.

773 Des. A 773. Des. B 773 Des. H 773 Des. M 773 Des. L 773 Des. G

PIN BOX (1¾" × 2¾" × 3⅝") Price $ 0.20 each $ 2.⁰⁰ p.doz.

548 Des. N 548 Des. E 548 Des. M 548 Des. F 548 Des. L 548 Des. G

CORD BOX (2¼" × 3") Price $ 0.20 each $ 2.⁰⁰ p.doz.

568 Des. C 568 Des. O 568 Des. P 568 Des. L 568 Des. G

CARD BOX (2" × 3¾" × 4¾") Price $ 0.50 each $ 6.⁰⁰ p.doz.

631 Des. B 631 Des. H 631 Des. N
BON BON BOX (1½" × 2⅝")
Price $ 0.20 each $ 2.⁰⁰ p.doz.

569 Des. J
STUD BOX

631 Des. M 631 Des. C 631 Des. G
BON BON BOX (1½" × 2⅝")
Price $ 0.20 each $ 2.⁰⁰ p.doz.

932 Des. A 932 Des. M 932 Des. C
JEWEL BOX (2" × 3½")
Price $ 0.35 each $ 4.⁰⁰ p.doz.

569 Des. B
STUD BOX

932 Des. H 932 Des. L 932 Des. G
JEWEL BOX (2" × 3½")
Price $ 0.35 each $ 4.⁰⁰ p.doz.

567 Des. E 567 Des. D
PIN BOX (2" × 3" × 5½")
Price $ 0.50 each $ 6.⁰⁰ p.doz.

569 Des. C
STUD BOX (2¼" × 3¾" × 3¾")
Pr $ 0.50 each $ 6.⁰⁰ p.doz.

567 Des. A 567 Des. G
PIN BOX (2" × 3" × 5½")
Price $ 0.50 each $ 6.⁰⁰ p.doz.

725 *Des. W.*   725 *Des. T.*   725 *Des. L.*   725 *Des. X.*   725 *Des. G.*

Playing Card Box (1¼" × 3½" × 4")   Price $ 0.25 each $.3.⁰⁰ p.doz.   *Playing Card Box* (1¼ × 3½ × 4")

  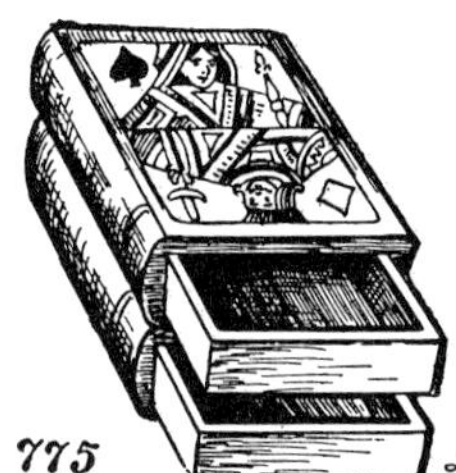  

775 *Des. T.*   775 *Des. W.*   775 *Des. Q. J.*   775 *Des. Y.*   775 *Des. G.*

Playing Card Box (double) (2¼" × 3½" × 4")   Pr. $ 0.35 each $ 4.⁰⁰ p.doz.   *Playing Card Box* (double) (2¼" × 3½" × 4")

710 *Des. G.* (2" × 3½" × 6") 710 *Des. K.*   546 *Des Y* (2¼" × 5" × 7½") 546 *Des. W.*

Card and Chip Box. Pr. $ 0.70 each   *Card & Chip Box* Empty Pr. $ 0.50 each $ 6.⁰⁰ p.doz.

(Cards & Chips included) $ 8.⁰⁰ p.doz.   Cards & Chips included Pr. $ 1.80 each $ 21.20 p.doz.

774 *Des. V* (3" × 9" × 12")

Card and Chip Box Empty Pr. $ 0.70 each $ 8.⁰⁰ p.doz.

Cards & Chips included Pr. $ 2.75 each $ 32.⁰⁰ p.doz.

761 *Des. G.* (4¼" × 5" × 8¼")

Card & Chip Box Empty Pr. $ 2.⁰⁰ each $ 24.⁰⁰ p.doz.

Cards & Chips included Pr. $ 4.⁰⁰ each $ 48.⁰⁰ p.doz.

 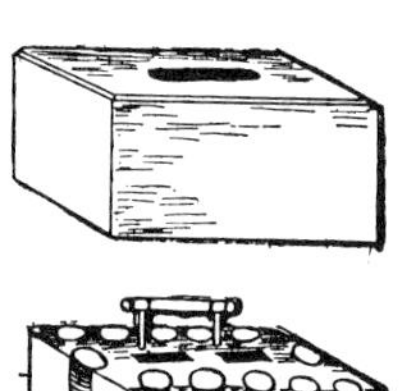 

965 *Des. B.* (4¾" × 7" × 10")

Chip Rack Empty Pr. $ 3.⁰⁰ each $ 36.⁰⁰ p.doz.

Cards & Chips included Pr. $ 5.⁰⁰ each $ 60.⁰⁰ p.doz.

758 *Des P* (4¾" × 6¼" × 8½")

Chip Rack Empty Pr. $ 4.⁰⁰ each $ 48.⁰⁰ p.doz.

Cards & Chips included Pr. $ 7.⁰⁰ each $ 84.⁰⁰ p.doz.

1039 Des. A.

1039 Des. M

1039 Des. G.

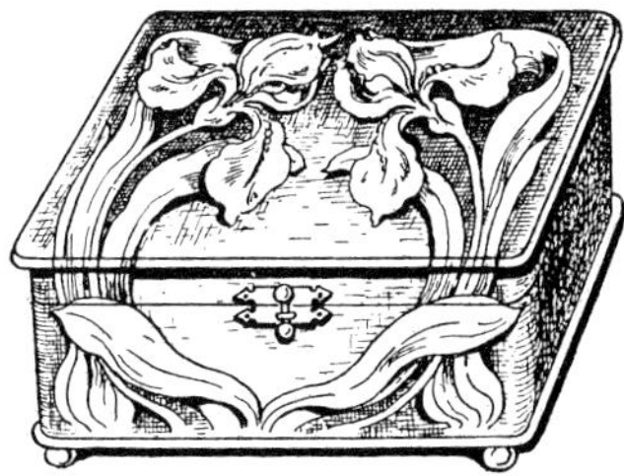

1039 Des. P.

WORK BOX (3½" × 6" × 7⅞") Price $ 0.50 each $ 6.ºº p.doz

1050 Des. S.

1050 Des. G.

1050 Des. J.

CIGAR BOX (4¼" × 6½" × 9¾") Fitted with patent metal lining and moistener
Price $ 1.85 each $ 16.ºº p.doz

1071 Des. B. (8½" × 12½")

1057 Des. N.

1071 Des. G. (8½" × 12½")

1057 Des. G.

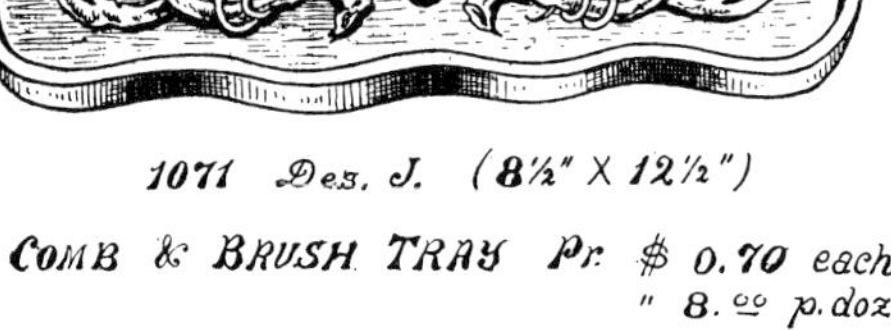

1071 Des. J. (8½" × 12½")

COMB & BRUSH TRAY Pr. $ 0.70 each
" 8.ºº p.doz.

1057 Des. E.

CALL BELL (3¾" inch)
Price $ 0.50 each
6.ºº p.doz.

1071 Des. K. (8½" × 12½")

COMB & BRUSH TRAY Pr. $ 0.70 each
8.ºº p.doz.

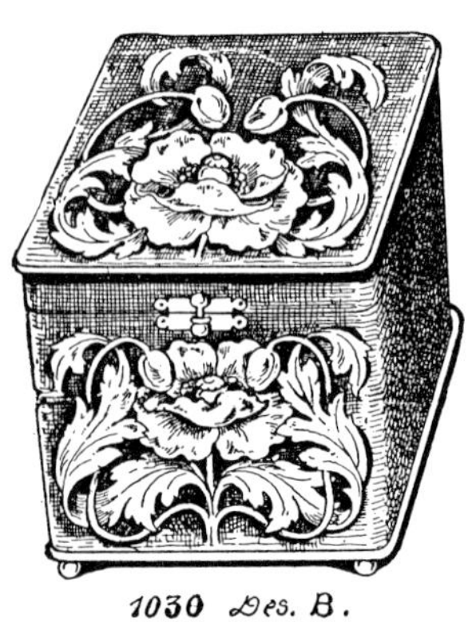

1030 *Des. B.*

1030 *Des. G.*

1030 *Des. A.*

1030 *Des. J*

COLLAR AND CUFF BOX (6⅜″ x 6⅜″ x 5½″) Price $ 0.50 each $ 6.⁰⁰ p.doz.

1038 *Des. C.*   (8⅜″ x 8⅜″ x 5⅝″)

COLLAR AND CUFF BOX 1038 *Des. K.*   Price $ 0.75 each
Pr. $ 9.⁰⁰ p.doz.

1038 *Des. G.*   (8⅜″ x 8⅜″ x 5⅝″)

1037 *Des. F.*

1037 *Des. D*

1037 *Des. L.*

PHOTO. BOX (7⅞″ x 15¼″ x 3⅞″) Price $ 1.⁰⁰ each
" 12.⁰⁰ p.doz.

1037 *Des. A.*

PHOTO. BOX (7⅞″ x 15¼″ x 3⅞″) Price $ 1.⁰⁰ each
" 12.⁰⁰ p.doz.

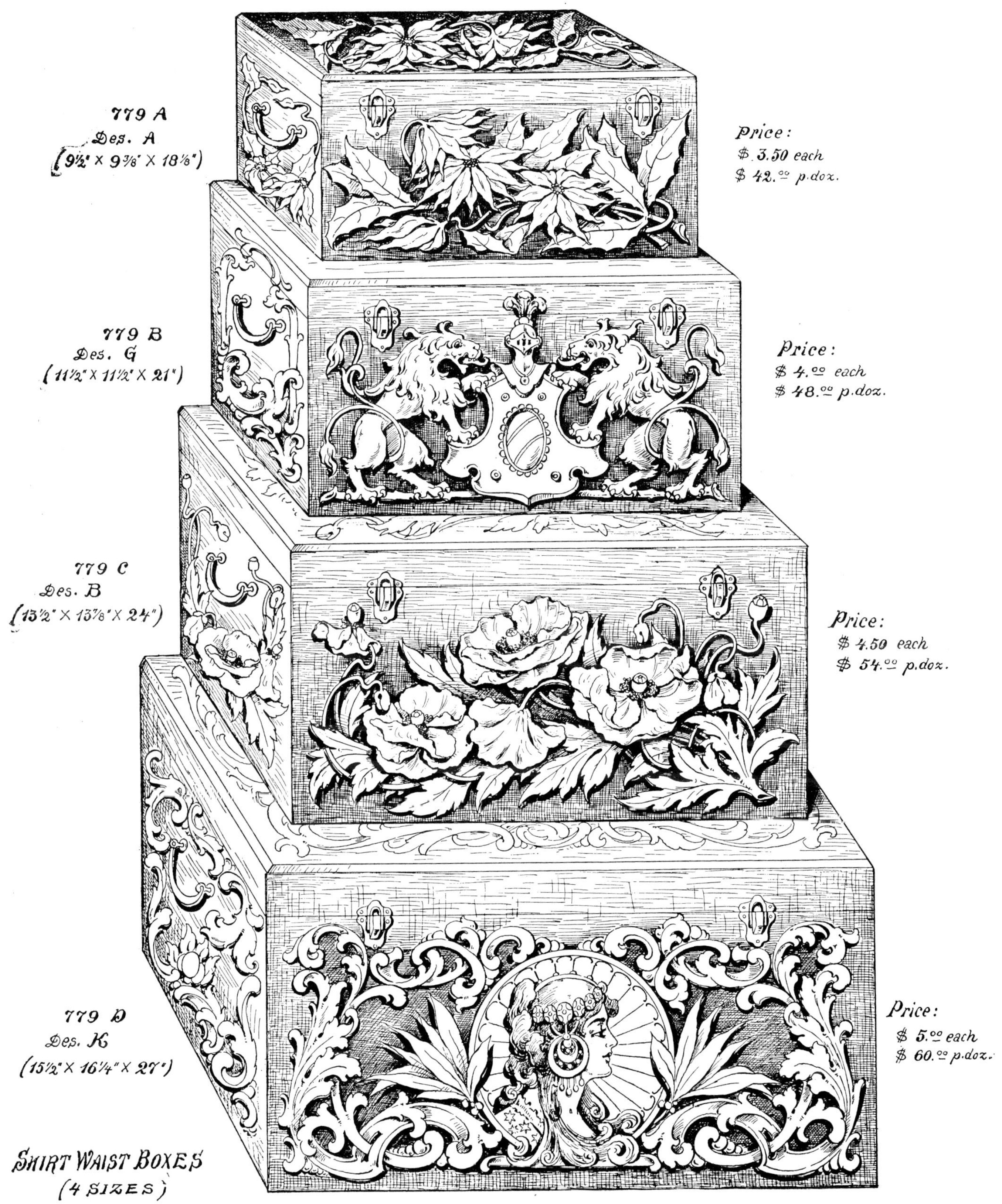

779 A
Des. A
(9½" × 9⅜" × 18⅞")
Price:
$ 3.50 each
$ 42.⁰⁰ p. doz.
779 B
Des. G
(11½" × 11½" × 21")
Price:
$ 4.⁰⁰ each
$ 48.⁰⁰ p. doz.
779 C
Des. B
(13½" × 13⅞" × 24")
Price:
$ 4.50 each
$ 54.⁰⁰ p. doz.
779 D
Des. K
(15½" × 16¼" × 27")
Price:
$ 5.⁰⁰ each
$ 60.⁰⁰ p. doz.
SHIRT WAIST BOXES
(4 SIZES)

THREE-PLY BASSWOOD FRAMES FITTED WITH GLASS & WIRE EASEL
Price $ 0.25 each $ 3.⁰⁰ p.doz.

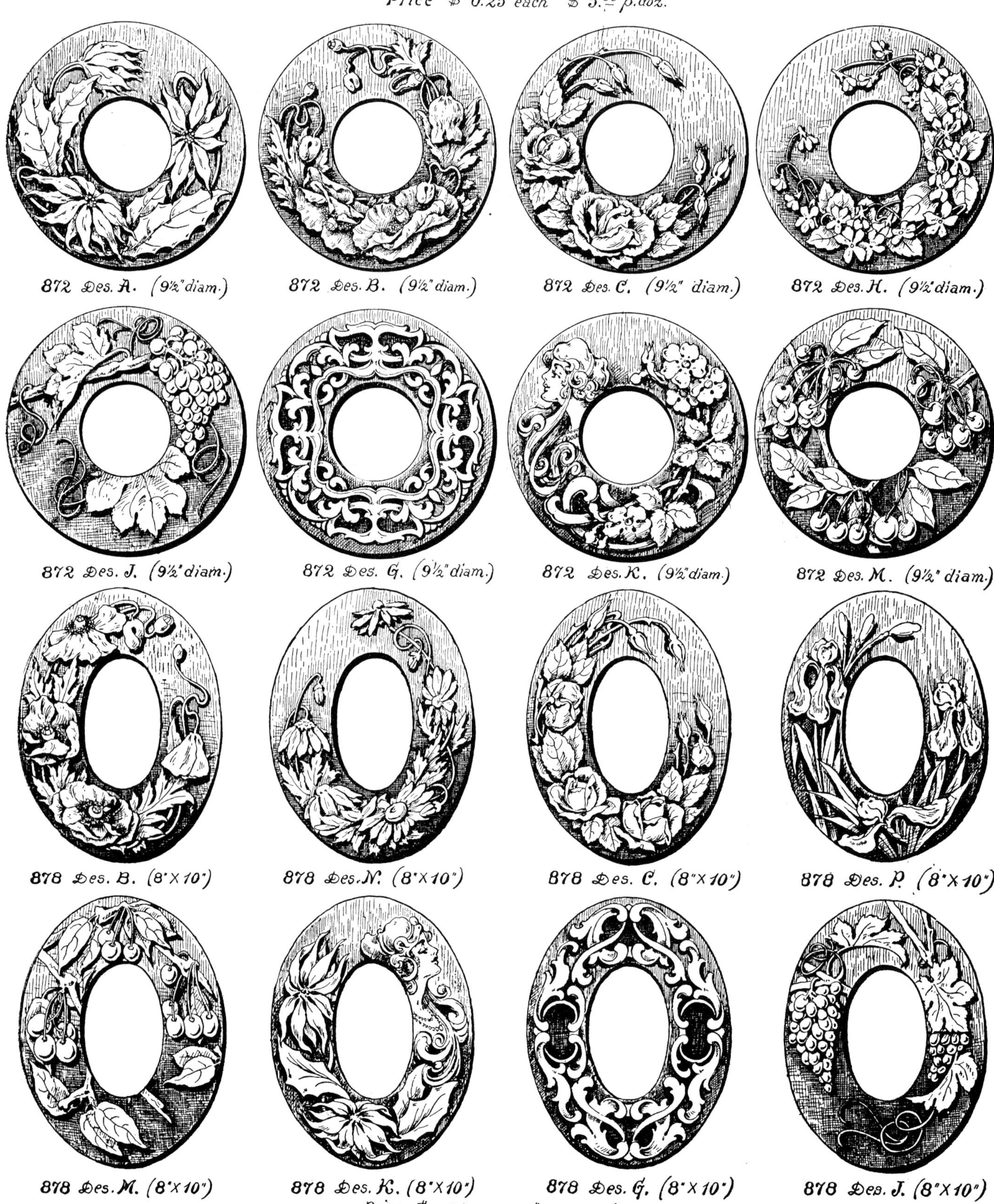

872 Des. A. (9½" diam.)   872 Des. B. (9½" diam.)   872 Des. C. (9½" diam.)   872 Des. H. (9½" diam.)

872 Des. J. (9½" diam.)   872 Des. G. (9½" diam.)   872 Des. K. (9½" diam.)   872 Des. M. (9½" diam.)

878 Des. B. (8"×10")   878 Des. N. (8"×10")   878 Des. C. (8"×10")   878 Des. P. (8"×10")

878 Des. M. (8"×10")   878 Des. K. (8"×10")   878 Des. G. (8"×10")   878 Des. J. (8"×10")

Price $ 0.25 each $ 3.⁰⁰ p.doz.

THREE-PLY BASSWOOD FRAMES FITTED WITH GLASS & WIRE EASEL
Price $ 0.25 each $ 2.80 p. doz.

874 Des. A.   (7½" × 9")   874 Des. B.   (7½" × 9")   874 Des. P.   (7½" × 9")   874 Des. D.   (7½" × 9")

874 Des. J.   (7½" × 9")   874 Des. H.   (7½" × 9")   874 Des. K.   (7½" × 9")   874 Des. M.   (7½" × 9")

875 Des. A.   (7½" × 9")   875 · Des. B.   (7½" × 9")   875 Des. C.   (7½" × 9")   875. Des. F.   (7½" × 9")

875 Des. J.   (7½" × 9")   875 Des. G.   (7½" × 9")   875 Des. K.   (7½" × 9")   875 Des. M.   (7½" × 9")

Price $ 0.25 each $ 2.80 p. doz.

THREE-PLY BASSWOOD FRAMES FITTED WITH GLASS & WIRE EASEL
873   Price $0.25 each $3.00 p.doz.

873 Des. A. (7½"×10")   873 Des. B. (7½"×10")   873 Des. C. (7½"×10")   873 Des. N. (7½"×10")

873 Des. J. (7½"×10")   873 Des. G (7½"×10")   873 Des. K. (7½"×10")   873 Des. M. (7½"×10")

948 Des. A. (9"×12")   948 Des. K. (9"×12")   948 Des. C. (9"×12")

948 Des. B. (9"×12")   948 Des. G. (9"×12")   948 Des. J. (9"×12")

948 Price $0.35 each $4.00 p.doz.

500
Round Frame
7 inch

Price, Each 30c.;
Doz., $3.20

502
Carte Frame
5⅜ x 4¾ in

Price, Each 25c.;
Doz., $2.50

501
Round Frame
7 inch

Price, Each 30c.;
Doz., $3.20

503
Carte Frame
5⅜ x 4¾ in

Price, Each 25c.;
Doz., $2.50

504
Rococo Frame
6¼ x 5½ in

Price, Each 25c.;
Doz., $3.00

507
Medium Cabinet Frame
7½ x 6 in

Price, Each 30c.;
Doz., $3.20

508
Medium Cabinet Frame
7½ x 6 in

Price, Each 30c.;
Doz., $3.20

509
Medium Cabinet Frame
7½ x 6 in

Price, Each 30c.;
Doz., $3.20

519
Turtle Frame
9½ x 6 in

Price, Each 35c.;
Doz., $4.00

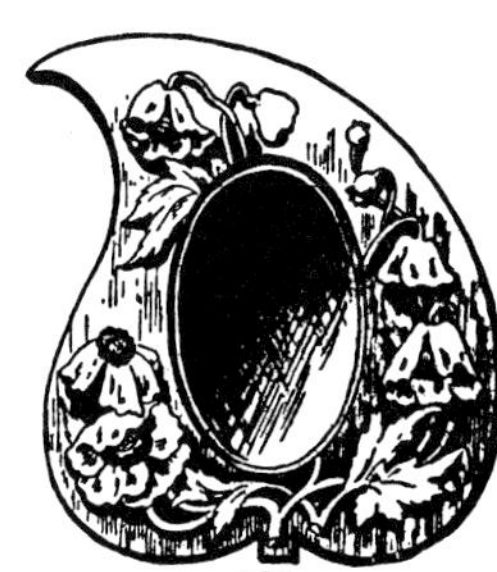

526
Leaf Frame
9 x 8½ in

Price, Each 35c.;
Doz., $4.00

510
Medium Cabinet Frame
7½ x 6 in

Price, Each 30c.;
Doz., $3.20

511
Medium Cabinet Frame
7½ x 6 in

Price, Each 30c.;
Doz., $3.20

512
Medium Cabinet Frame
7½ x 6 in

Price, Each 30c.;
Doz., $3.20

547
Fluted Frame
7¼ x 5⅜ in

Price, Each 30c.;
Doz., $3.60

536
Cabinet Frame
9½ x 8 in.

Price, Each 40c.;
Doz., $4.80

538
Cabinet Frame
10 x 7½ in

Price, Each 40c.; Doz., $4.80

506
Round Frame
9½ inch

Price, Each 30c.; Doz., $3.60

505
Round Frame
9½ inch

Price, Each 30c.; Doz., $3.60

537
Cabinet Frame
10 x 8 in.

Price, Each 40c.; Doz., $4.80

997 9¾" × 13⅞'
Price, 60c. Each; $7.00 Doz.

991 5½" × ⁷⅝'
25c. Each; $3.00 Doz.

994 7⅝' × 12⅜'
Price, 40c. Each; $4.50 Doz.

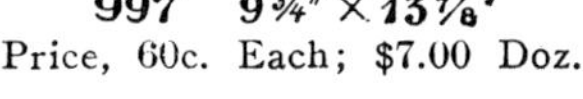

999 10½" × 13¼"
Price 70c. Each; $8.00 Doz.

992 6⅞×9"
30c. Each; $3.50 Doz.

993 8¼' × 10⅝'
35c. Each; $4.00 Doz.

996 8¾ × 14¼'
Price 50c. Each; $6.00 Doz.

998 7⅝" × 17⅜"
Price 70c. Each; $8.00 Doz.

1000 11" × 14½'
Price 70c. Each; $8.00 Doz.

995 8⅛ × 13⅛"
Price 45c. Each; $5.00 Doz.

1001 11⅝" × 15¾'
Price 70c. Each; $8.00 Doz.

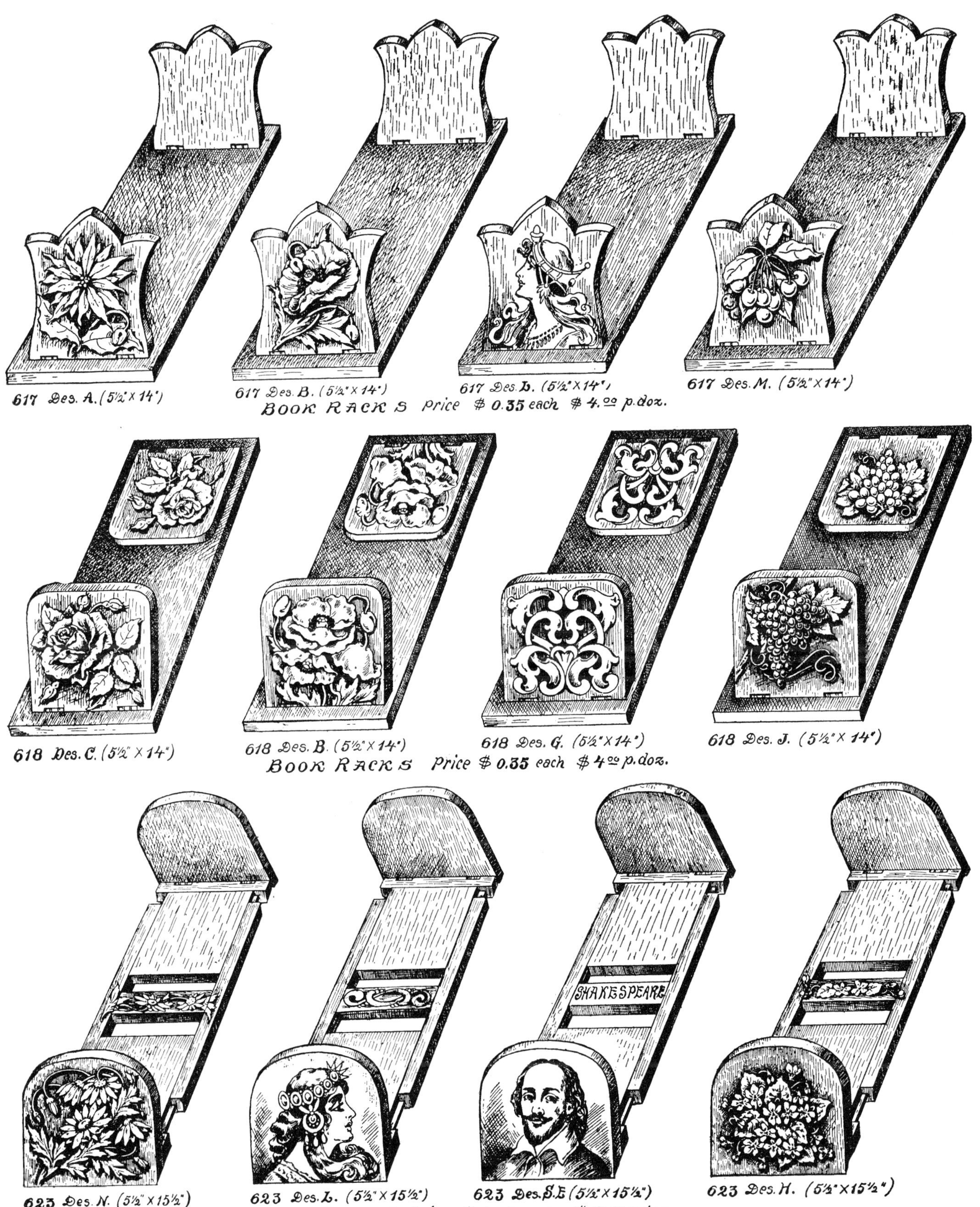

617 Des. A. (5½" × 14") 617 Des. B. (5½" × 14") 617 Des. D. (5½" × 14") 617 Des. M. (5½" × 14")

BOOK RACKS Price $ 0.35 each $ 4.00 p. doz.

618 Des. C. (5½" × 14") 618 Des. B. (5½" × 14") 618 Des. G. (5½" × 14") 618 Des. J. (5½" × 14")

BOOK RACKS Price $ 0.35 each $ 4.00 p. doz.

623 Des. N. (5½" × 15½") 623 Des. L. (5½" × 15½") 623 Des. S.E (5½" × 15½") 623 Des. H. (5½" × 15½")

BOOK RACKS Price $ 0.70 each $ 8.00 p. doz.

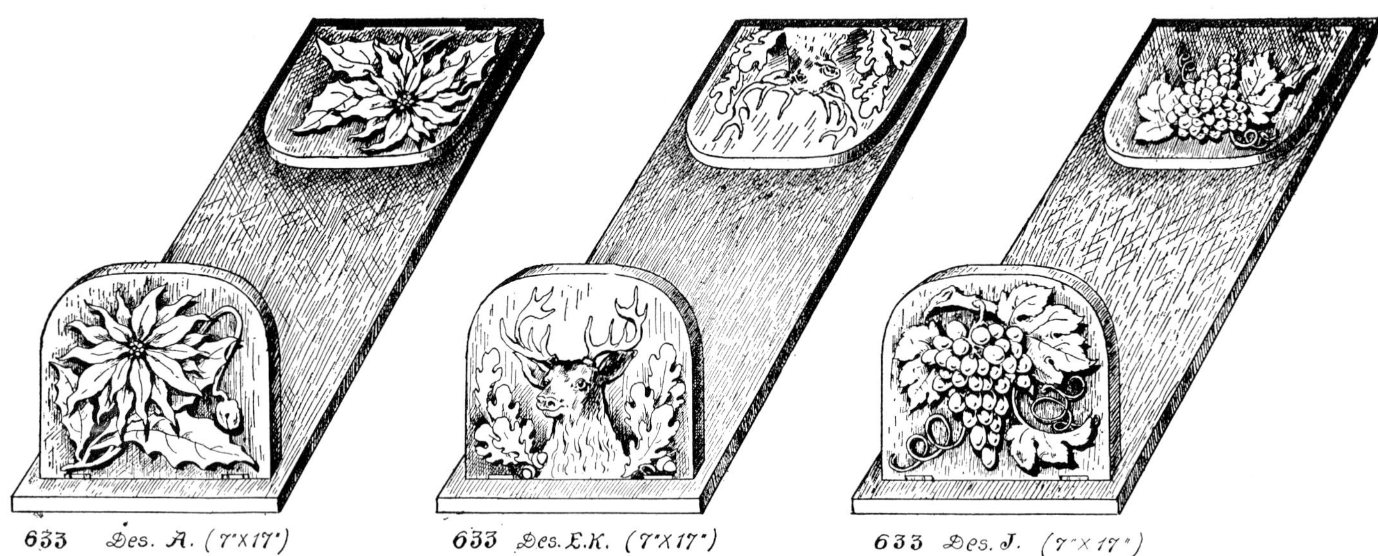

633 Des. A. (7"x17")   633 Des. E.K. (7"x17")   633 Des. J. (7"x17")

BOOK RACKS Price $ 0.50 each $ 6.00 p.doz.

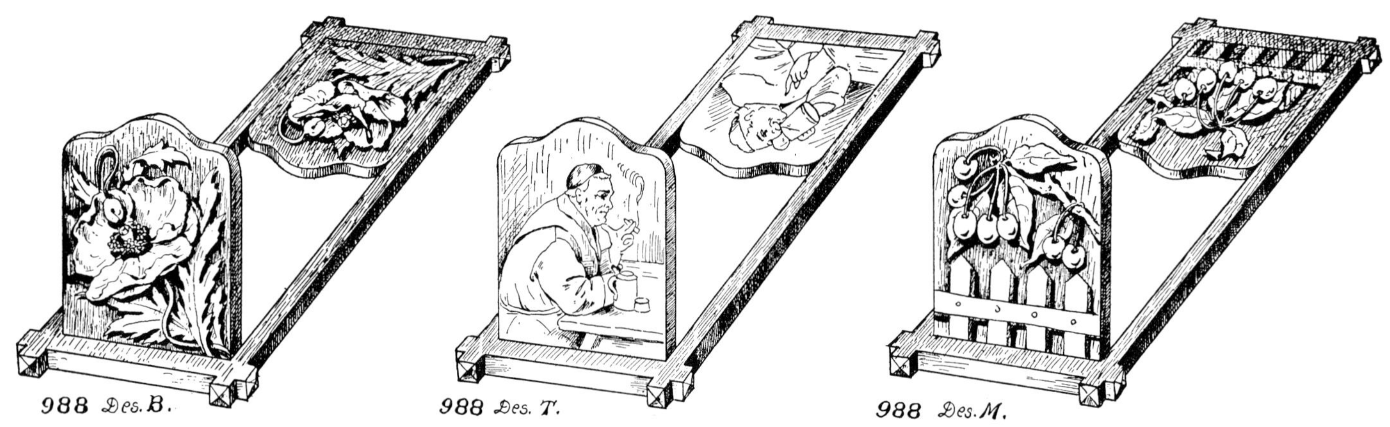

988 Des. B.   988 Des. T.   988 Des. M.

BOOK RACKS Price $ 0.35 each $ 4.00 p.doz.

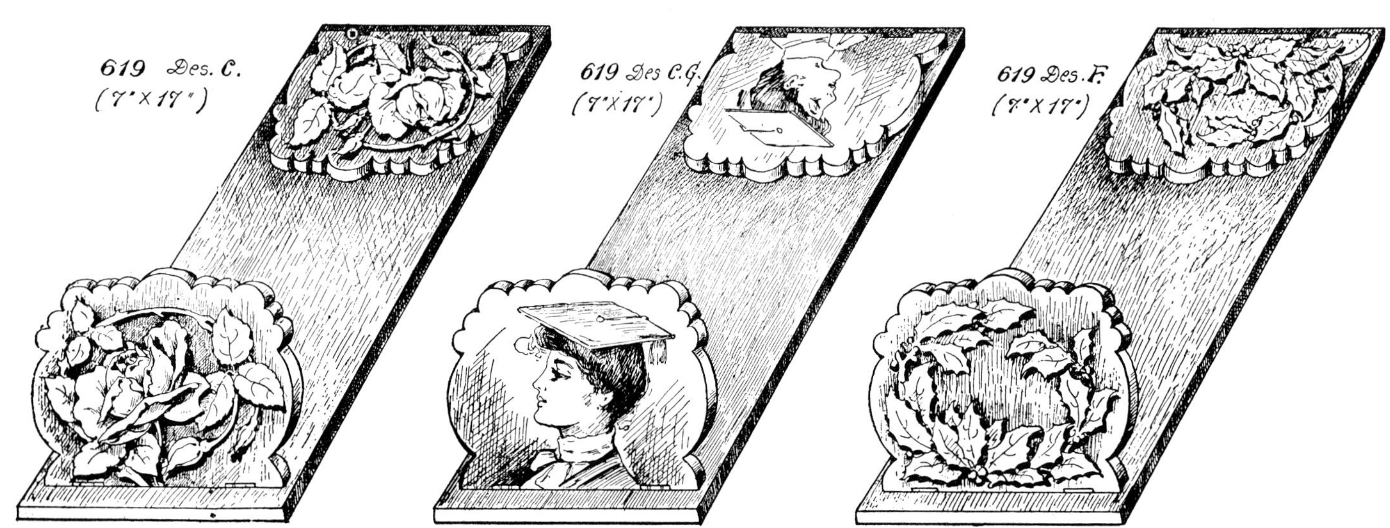

619 Des. C.   619 Des. C.G.   619 Des. F.
(7"x17")   (7"x17")   (7"x17")

BOOK RACKS Price $ 0.50 each $ 6.00 p.doz.

(54)

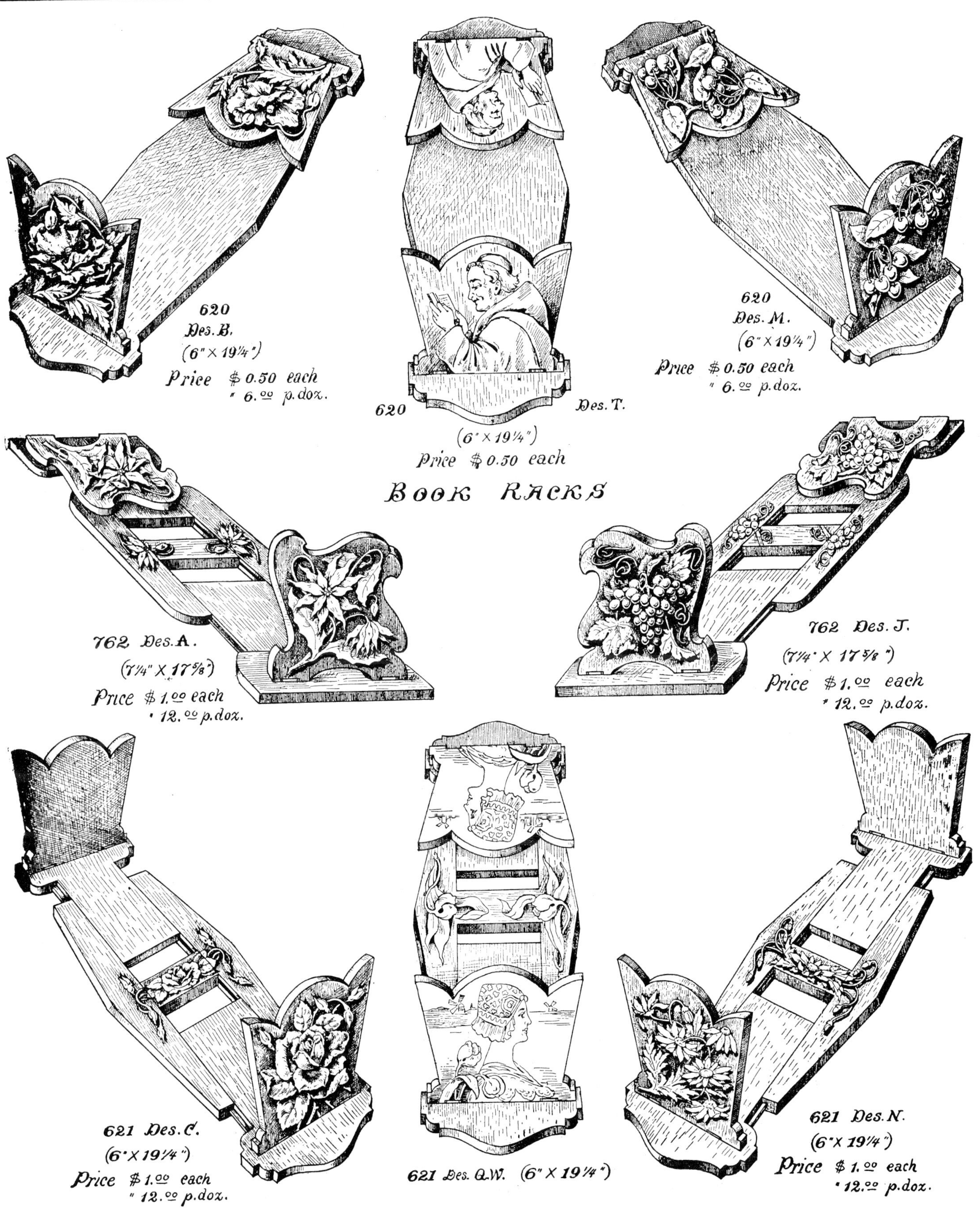

620
Des. B.
(6" × 19¼")
Price $ 0.50 each
" 6.⁰⁰ p. doz.

620
Des. T.
(6" × 19¼")
Price $ 0.50 each

620
Des. M.
(6" × 19¼")
Price $ 0.50 each
" 6.⁰⁰ p. doz.

BOOK RACKS

762 Des. A.
(7¼" × 17⅝")
Price $ 1.⁰⁰ each
· 12.⁰⁰ p. doz.

762 Des. J.
(7¼" × 17⅝")
Price $ 1.⁰⁰ each
" 12.⁰⁰ p. doz.

621 Des. C.
(6" × 19¼")
Price $ 1.⁰⁰ each
" 12.⁰⁰ p. doz.

621 Des. Q.W. (6" × 19¼")

621 Des. N.
(6" × 19¼")
Price $ 1.⁰⁰ each
· 12.⁰⁰ p. doz.

622 Des. B.
(7" × 19")   Price $ 1.00 each
" 12.00 p. doz.

622 Des. P. H.   (7" × 19")
Price $ 1.00 each
" 12.00 p. doz.

BOOK RACKS

622 Des. C.
(7" × 19")   Price $ 1.00 each
" 12.00 p. doz.

634 Des. A. (7" × 19")   634. Des. J.   (7" × 19")
Price $ 0.75 each
" 9.00 p. doz.

BOOK RACKS

634 Des. G.
(7" × 19")
Price $ 0.75 each
" 9.00 p. doz

634 Des. L.
(7" × 19")
Price $ 0.75 each
" 9.00 p. doz.

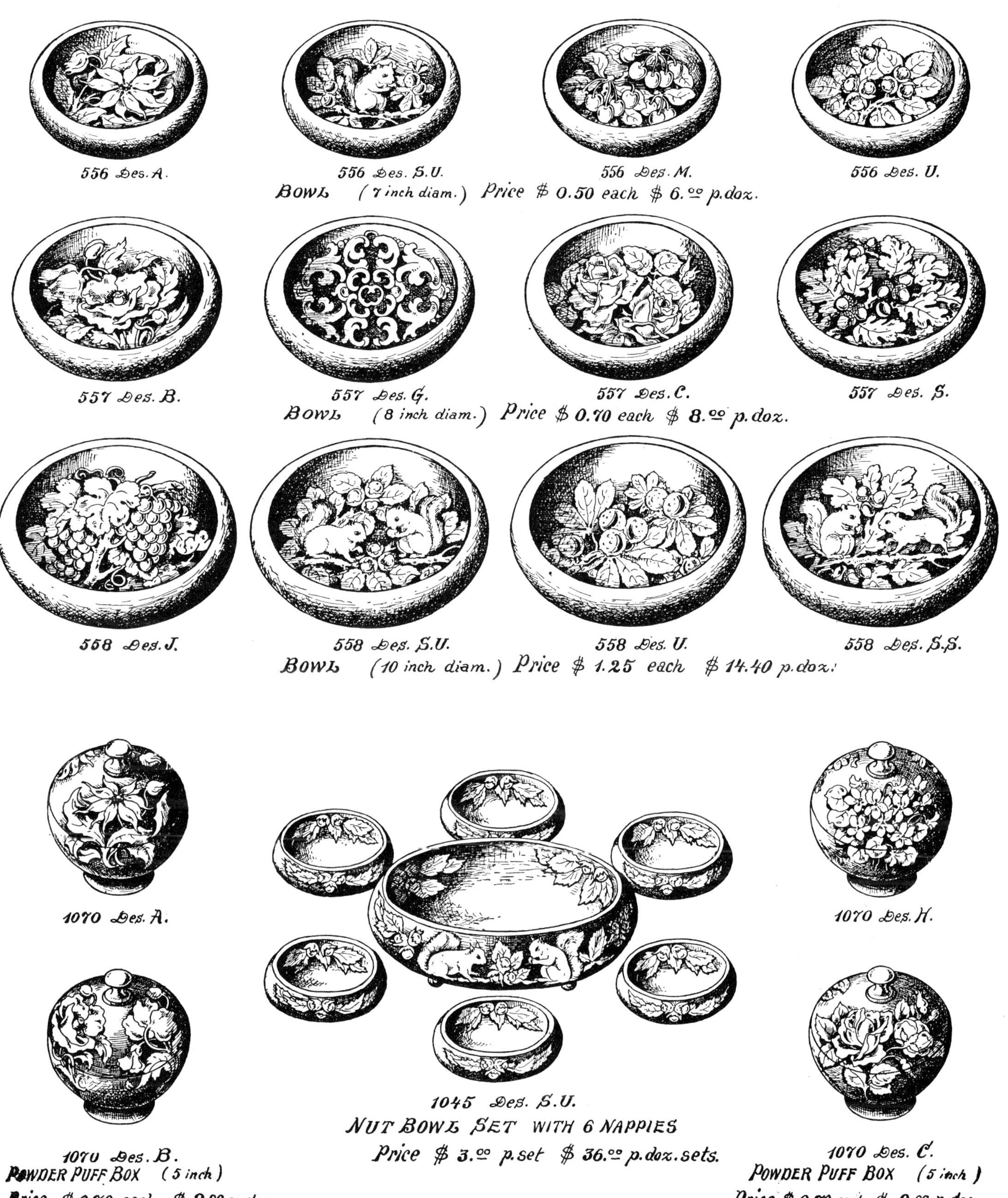

556 Des. A.   556 Des. S.U.   556 Des. M.   556 Des. U.

BOWL   (7 inch diam.)   Price $ 0.50 each $ 6.⁰⁰ p.doz.

557 Des. B.   557 Des. G.   557 Des. C.   557 Des. S.

BOWL   (8 inch diam.)   Price $ 0.70 each $ 8.⁰⁰ p.doz.

558 Des. J.   558 Des. S.U.   558 Des. U.   558 Des. S.S.

BOWL   (10 inch diam.)   Price $ 1.25 each $ 14.40 p.doz.

1070 Des. A.   1070 Des. H.

1045 Des. S.U.

NUT BOWL SET WITH 6 NAPPIES

Price $ 3.⁰⁰ p.set $ 36.⁰⁰ p.doz. sets.

1070 Des. B.
POWDER PUFF BOX   (5 inch)
Price $ 0.70 each $ 8.⁰⁰ p.doz.

1070 Des. C.
POWDER PUFF BOX   (5 inch)
Price $ 0.70 each $ 8.⁰⁰ p.doz.

1051 *Des. J.* (8 inch)
BOWL WITH COVER Pr. $ 1.35 each $ 16.⁰⁰ p. doz.

1051 *Des. M.* (8 inch)
BOWL WITH COVER Pr. $ 1.35 each $ 16.⁰⁰ p. doz.

816 *Des. M.*

816 *Des. H.*

BOWL (5 inch)
Price $ 0.25 each $ 3.⁰⁰ p. doz.

1051 *Des. S.S.* (8 inch)
BOWL WITH COVER
Price $ 1.35 each $ 16.⁰⁰ p. doz.

816 *Des. G.*

816 *Des. J.*

BOWL (5 inch)
Price $ 0.25 each $ 3.⁰⁰ p. doz.

1048 *Des. N.* (7 inch)

1048 *Des. J.* (7 inch)

BOWL
1048 *Des. M.* (7 inch)

1048 *Des. S.* (7 inch)

Price $ 0.80 each $ 9.60 p. doz.

1047 *Des. B.* (8 inch)

BOWL
1047 *Des. S.S.* (8 inch)

BOWL

1047 *Des. A.* (8 inch)

Price $ 1.⁰⁰ each $ 12.⁰⁰ p. doz.

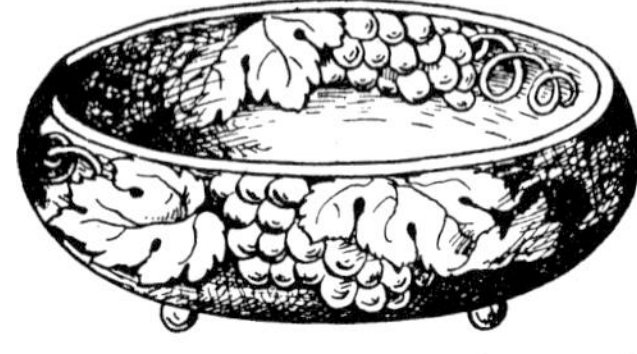

1046 *Des. J.* (9 inch)

BOWL
1046 *Des. U.* (9 inch)

BOWL

1046 *Des. G.* (9 inch)

Price $ 1.35 each $ 16.⁰⁰ p. doz.

1081 *Des. S.O.* (10 inch)

BOWL
1081 *Des. B.* (10 inch)

BOWL

1081 *Des. M.* (10 inch)

Price $ 1.50 each $ 18.⁰⁰ p. doz.

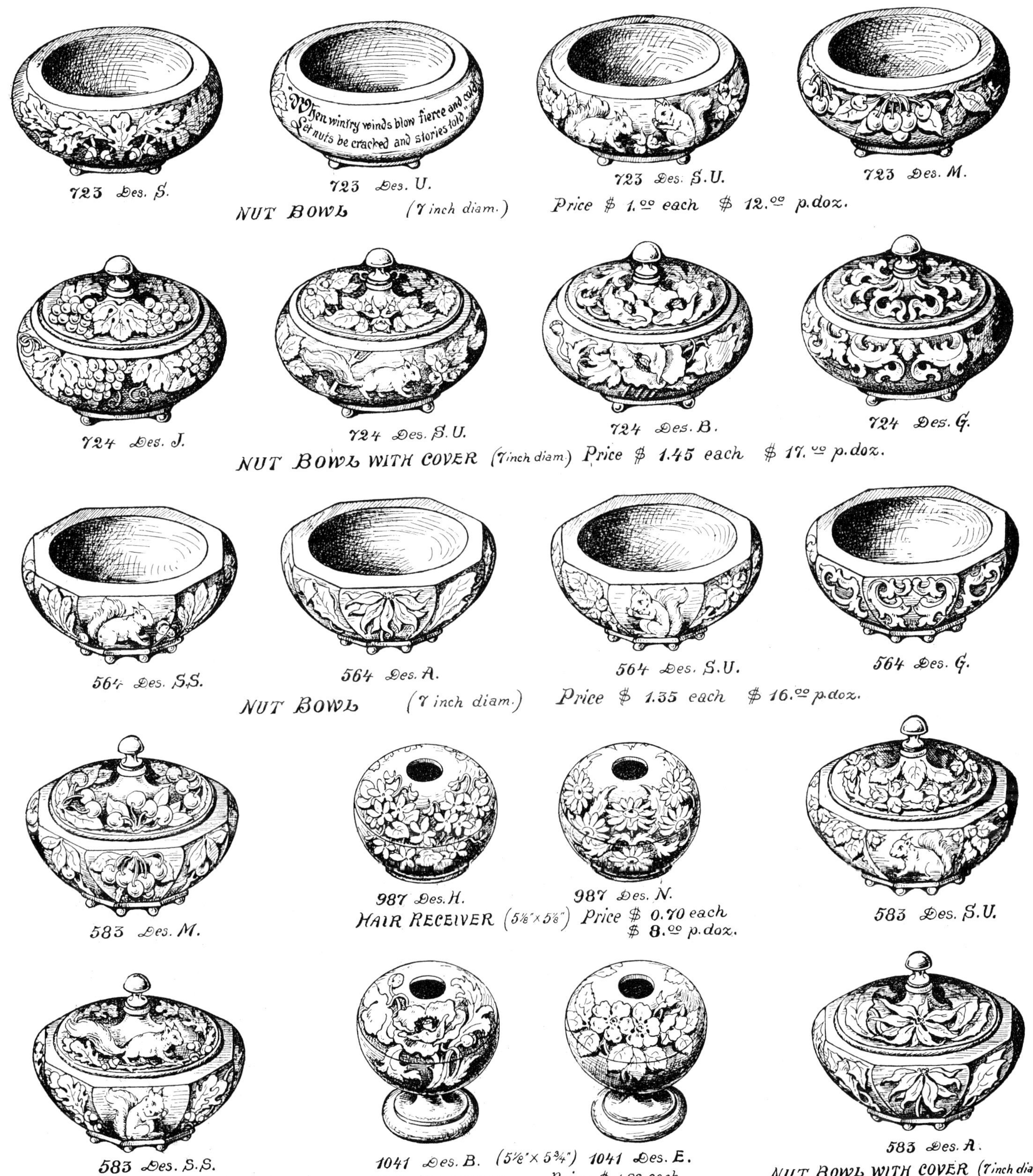

723 Des. S.   723 Des. U.   723 Des. S.U.   723 Des. M.

NUT BOWL   (7 inch diam.)   *Price $ 1.00 each $ 12.00 p. doz.*

724 Des. J.   724 Des. S.U.   724 Des. B.   724 Des. G.

NUT BOWL WITH COVER (7 inch diam.) *Price $ 1.45 each $ 17.00 p. doz.*

564 Des. S.S.   564 Des. A.   564 Des. S.U.   564 Des. G.

NUT BOWL   (7 inch diam.)   *Price $ 1.35 each $ 16.00 p. doz.*

583 Des. M.   987 Des. H.   987 Des. N.   583 Des. S.U.

HAIR RECEIVER (5⅛" × 5⅛") *Price $ 0.70 each
                               $ 8.00 p. doz.*

583 Des. S.S.   1041 Des. B. (5⅛" × 5¾") 1041 Des. E.   583 Des. A.

NUT BOWL WITH COVER (7 inch diam.)   *HAIR RECEIVER   Price $ 1.00 each   NUT BOWL WITH COVER* (7 inch diam.)
Price $ 1.75 each $ 20.00 p. doz.   *$ 12.00 p. doz.   Price $ 1.75 each $ 20.00 p. doz.*

EACH NUMBER FURNISHED IN THE FOLLOWING DESIGNS ONLY :
ANDOVER, AMHERST, BROWN, BOWDOIN, COLUMBIA, CORNELL, DARTMOUTH, HARVARD,
PRINCETON, SMITH, TUFTS, WESLEYAN, YALE, U. of PENNSYLVANIA, MASS. INSTITUTE of TECHNOLOGY.

854 COLL. Des. (15" diam.)
THREE PLY PANEL   Price $0.45 each
" 5.00 p. doz.

851 COLL. Des. (8" diam)
THREE PLY PANEL
Price $0.15 each
" 1.50 p. doz.

854 COLL. Des. (15" diam.)
THREE PLY PANEL   Price $0.45 each
" 5.00 p. doz.

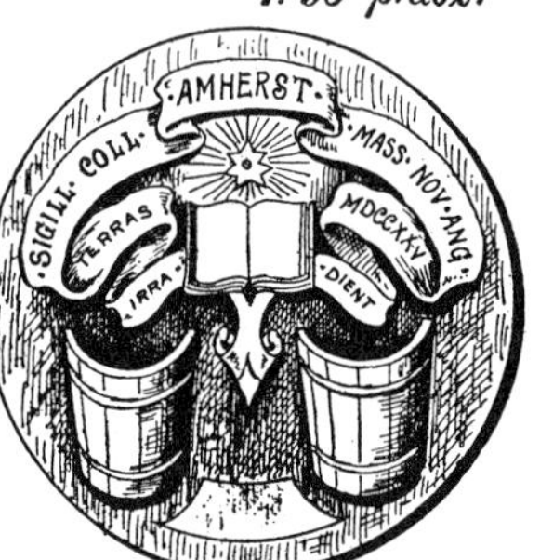

892 COLL. Des.
MATCH HOLDER (7" diam)
Price $0.35 each
" 4.00 p. doz.

650 COLL. Des. (9" X 16")
PIPE RACK   Price $0.50 each
" 6.00 p. doz.

584 COLL. Des. (2¼" X 6" X 8¼")
INKSTAND (2 inkwells) Pr. $0.50 each
" 6.00 p. doz.

715 COLL. Des.
ALARM CLOCK STAND (5½" X 10½")
Price (without works) $0.70 each $8.40 p. doz.
(with works) $2.00 " $24.00 "

643 COLL. Des.
WASTE BASKET (9½" X 18")
Price $1.25 each
" 14.40 p. doz.

641 COLL. Des.
WASTE BASKET (8½" X 13¾")
Price $0.70 each
" 8.00 p. doz.

EACH NUMBER FURNISHED IN THE FOLLOWING DESIGNS ONLY :
ANDOVER, AMHERST, BROWN, BOWDOIN, COLUMBIA, CORNELL, DARTMOUTH, HARVARD,
PRINCETON. SMITH, TUFTS, WESLEYAN, YALE, U. of PENNSYLVANIA, MASS. INSTITUTE of TECHNOLOGY.

604 *COLL. Des.*
BROOM HOLDER (5½"x11")
Price $ 0.25 each
" 3.00 p.doz.

735 *COLL. Des.*
STEIN RACK AND SHELF (11"x19½") *Pr.* $ 1.35 each
" 15.60 p.doz.

561 COLL. Des.
TOBACCO JAR (4¾"X 5½")
Price $ 1.25 each
" 14.40 p.doz.

743 *COLL. Des.*
TIE OR TOWEL RACK (9"X21") *Price* $0.50 each
" 6.00 p.doz.

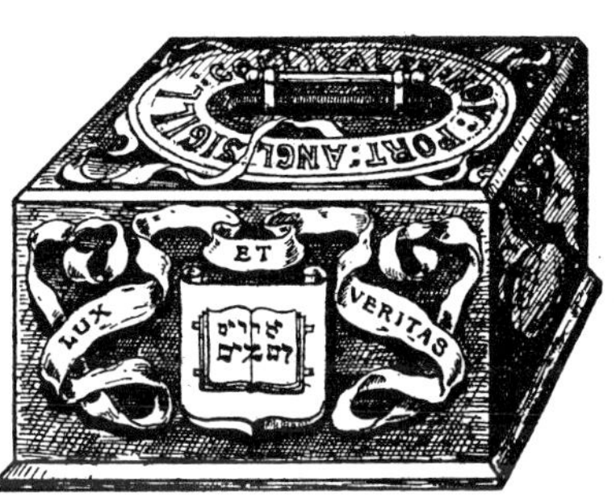

965 COLL. Des. (4¾"X7"X10")
CHIP BOX (for 300 chips & 2 pack cards)
Pr. empty $ 3.00 each $ 36.00 p.doz.
CARDS & CHIPS included $ 5.00 each
$ 60.00 p.doz.

622 COLL. Des. (7"X19")
BOOK RACK *Pr.* $ 1.00 each
" 12.00 p.doz.

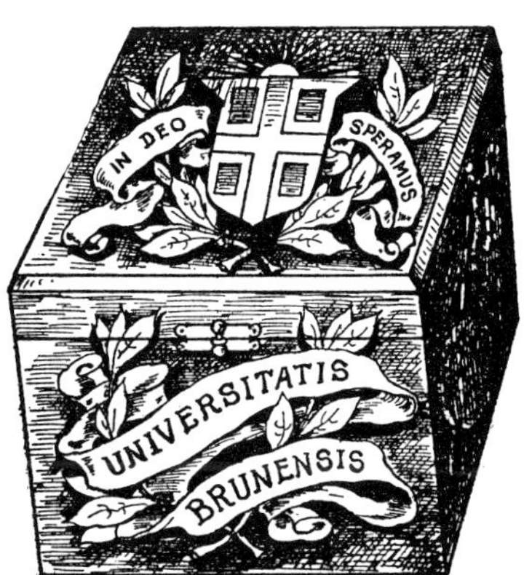

931 COLL. Des. (6"X8"X8")
COLLAR & CUFF BOX
Price $ 0.70 each
" 8.00 p.doz.

551 COLL. Des.
THERMOMETER (7"X16½")
Price $0.80 each $ 9.60 p.doz.

889 Des. G   (7" x 14")

889 Des. V.   (7" x 14")

889 Des. J.   (7" x 14")

PIPE RACKS   price $ 0.30 each $ 3.50 p. doz.

650   Des. V   (9" x 16")
PIPE RACK Pr. $ 0.50 each $ 6.00 p. doz.

651 Des. G   (7½" x 9¼")
PIPE RACK (standing)
Pr. $ 0.50 each $ 6.00 p. doz.

652 Des. T   (9½" x 16")
PIPE RACK WITH MATCH BOX Pr. $ 0.75 each
9.00 p. doz.

650   Des. G   (9" x 16")
PIPE RACK Pr. $ 0.50 each $ 6.00 p. doz.

651 Des. A   (7½" x 9¼")
PIPE RACK (standing)
Pr. $ 0.50 each $ 6.00 p. doz.

652 Des. D.S. (9½" x 16")
PIPE RACK WITH MATCH BOX Pr. $ 0.75 each
9.00 p. doz.

650   Des. S.M. (9" x 16")
PIPE RACK Pr. $ 0.50 each $ 6.00 p. doz.

651 Des. J   (7½" x 9¼")
PIPE RACK (standing)
Pr. $ 0.50 each $ 6.00 p. doz.

652 Des. G   (9½" x 16")
PIPE RACK WITH MATCH BOX Pr. $ 0.75 each $ 9.00 p. doz.

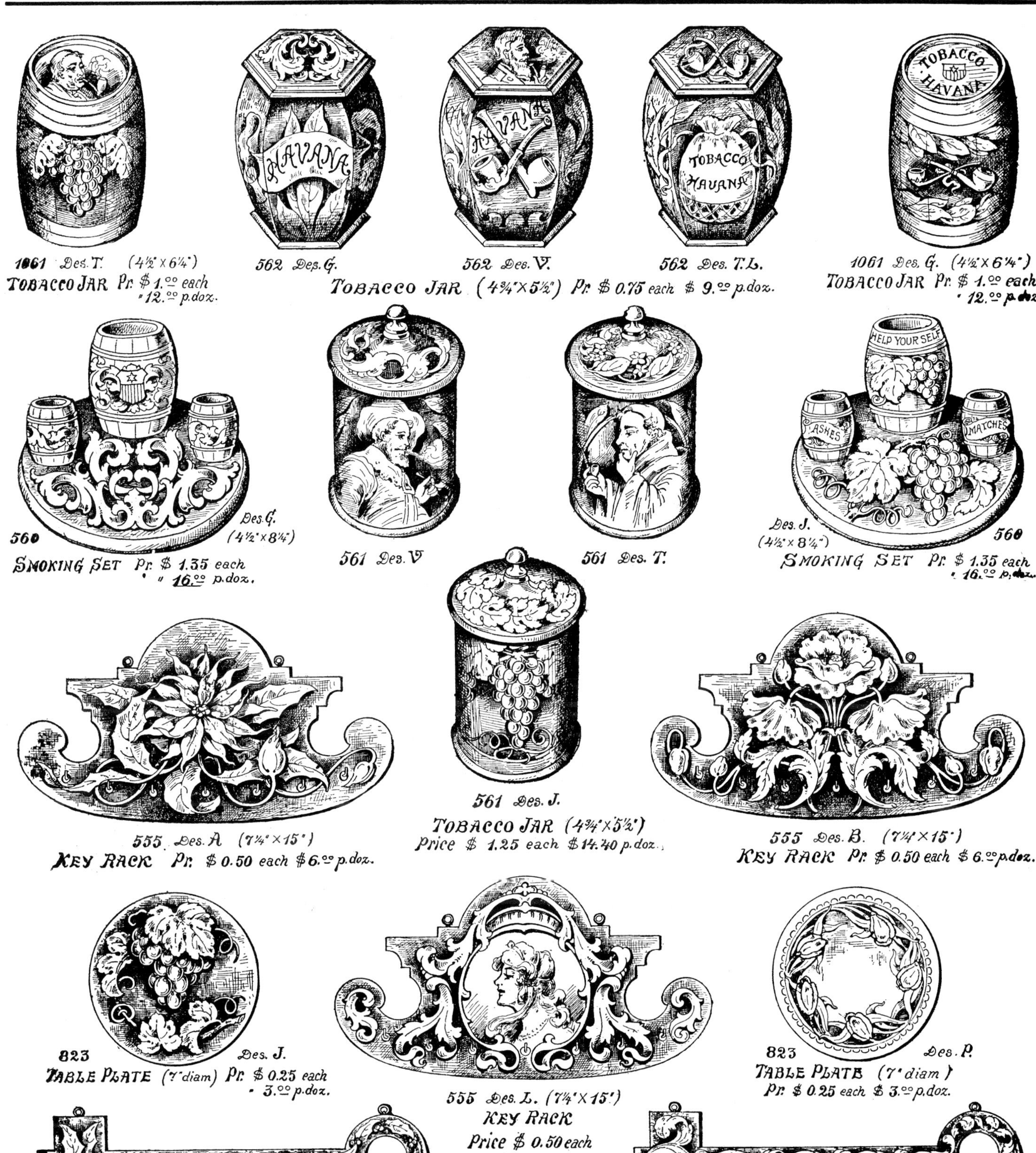

1061 Des. T. (4½"×6¼")
TOBACCO JAR Pr. $ 1.00 each
" 12.00 p.doz.

562 Des. G.

562 Des. V.

562 Des. T. L.

TOBACCO JAR (4¾"×5½") Pr. $ 0.75 each $ 9.00 p.doz.

1061 Des. G. (4½"×6¼")
TOBACCO JAR Pr. $ 1.00 each
" 12.00 p.doz.

560

Des. G.
(4½"×8¼")

SMOKING SET Pr. $ 1.35 each
" 16.00 p.doz.

561 Des. V

561 Des. T.

Des. J.
(4½"×8¼")

560

SMOKING SET Pr. $ 1.35 each
" 16.00 p.doz.

555 Des. A (7¼"×15")
KEY RACK Pr. $ 0.50 each $6.00 p.doz.

561 Des. J.
TOBACCO JAR (4¾"×5½")
Price $ 1.25 each $14.40 p.doz.

555 Des. B. (7¼"×15")
KEY RACK Pr. $ 0.50 each $6.00 p.doz.

823 Des. J.
TABLE PLATE (7" diam) Pr. $ 0.25 each
" 3.00 p.doz.

555 Des. L. (7¼"×15')
KEY RACK
Price $ 0.50 each
$ 6.00 p.doz.

823 Des. P.
TABLE PLATE (7" diam)
Pr. $ 0.25 each $ 3.00 p.doz.

554 Des. F. (4½"×15¼") KEY RACK
Price $ 0.35 each $ 4.00 p.doz.

554 Des. G. (4½"×15¼") KEY RACK
Price $ 0.35 each $ 4.00 p.doz.

727 Des. A

892 (7″ diam) Des. A
MATCH HOLDER Pr. $ 0.35 each
· 4.⁰⁰ p.doz.

899 (7″x 10″) Des. D.C.
MATCH HOLDER Pr. $ 0.35 each
· 4.⁰⁰ p.doz

785 Des. H

785 Des. G

785 Des. N.
MATCH HOLDER (4″x 5½″) Price $0.35 each
· 4.⁰⁰ p.doz.

727 Des. T

1042 (10⅜″ x 12½″) Des. D.C.

1042 (10⅜″ × 12½″) Des. D G
MATCH HOLDER & PIPE RACK Pr. $ 0.70 each
· 8 ⁰⁰ p.doz

727 Des. V

MATCH HOLDER (7½″x 7½″) Pr. $ 0.25 each $ 3.⁰⁰ p.doz.

727 Des. D.C.

892 (7″ diam) Des. V
MATCH HOLDER Pr. $ 0.35 each
· 4.⁰⁰ p.doz.

899 (7″x 10″) Des. A
MATCH HOLDER Pr. $ 0.35 each
· 4.⁰⁰ p.doz.

1004 Des. G

1004 Des. A

1004 Des. B
MATCH HOLDER (3¼″x 5¼″) Pr. $ 0 20 each
· 2.⁰⁰ p.doz.

250 250 250 250 250

250 BARK PANELS (assort JAPS des) Price $ 0.40 each
" 4.50 p.doz

1065 (5½" × 7½")
MATCH HOLDER Pr. $ 0.25 each
" 3.00 p.doz.

1069 (5" × 9¼")
MATCH HOLDER
Pr. $ 0.40 each
" 4.50 p.doz.

1067 (7½" × 12")
PIPE RACK & MATCH HOLDER
Pr. $ 0.40 each
" 4.50 p.doz.

1066 (7" × 12")
PIPE RACK & MATCH HOLDER
Pr. $ 0.35 each
" 4.00 p.doz.

1068 (5" × 12")
MATCH HOLDER
Pr. $ 0.40 each
" 4.50 p.doz.

1064 Des. A.B SKULL PIPE RACK (7¾" × 12")
Price $ 0.30 each $ 3.50 p.doz.

1072 (5½" × 11")
MATCH HOLDER Pr. $ 0.35 each
" 4.00 p.doz.

1064 Des. A.C. SKULL PIPE RACK (7¾" × 12")
Price $ 0.30 each $ 3.50 p.doz.

787 Des. B.   787 Des. M.
MATCH HOLDER (5"x 7")
Price $0.25 each $3.00 p.doz.

891 Des. L.H.   891 Des. Q.
MATCH HOLDER (4"x 11)
Price $0.30 each
" 3.50 p.doz.

787 Des. N.   787 Des. H.
MATCH HOLDER (5"x 7")
Price $0.25 each $3.00 p.doz.

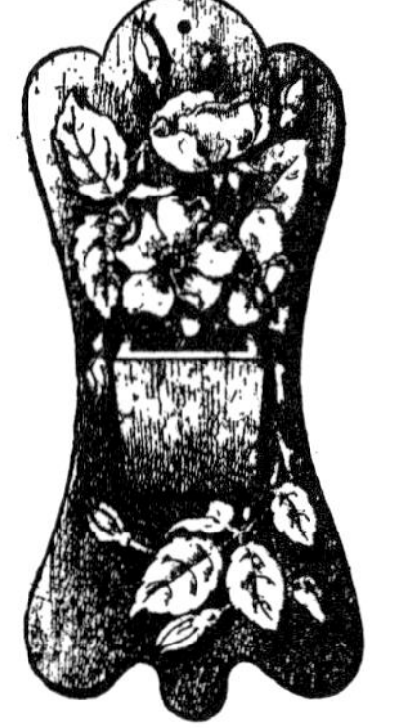

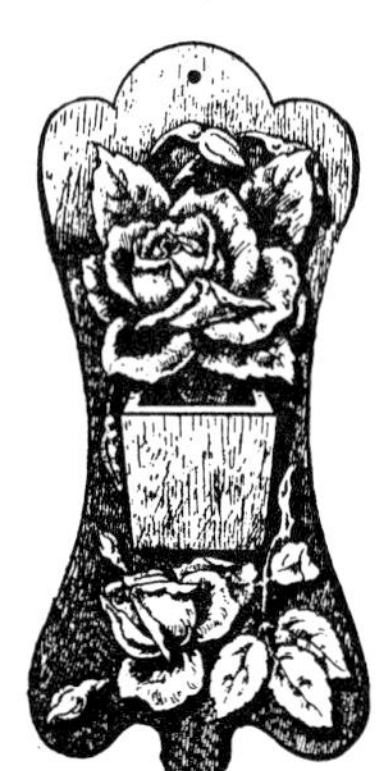

788 Des. E.   788 Des. C.
MATCH HOLDER (4½"x 10)
Price $0.25 each $3.00 p.doz.

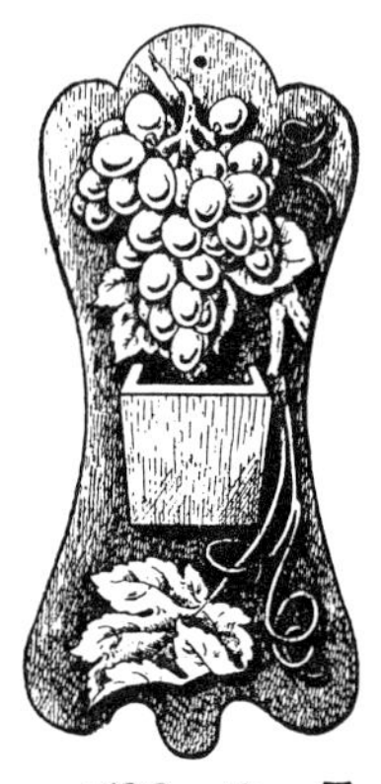

788 Des. J.   788 Des. G.
MATCH HOLDER (4½"x 10")
Price $0.25 each $3.00 p.doz.

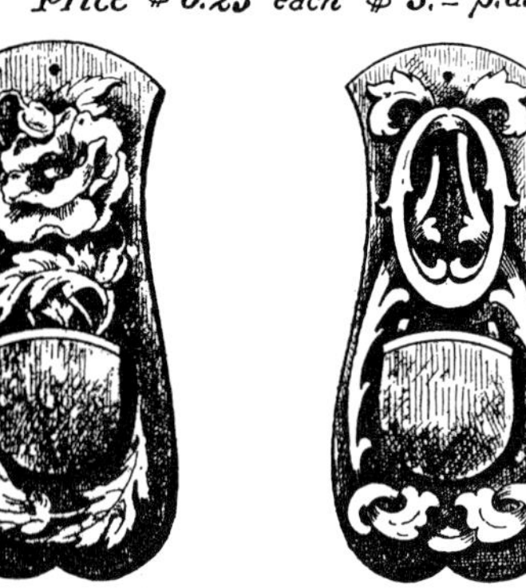

789 Des. R   789 Des. G.
MATCH HOLDER (4"x 9)
Price $0.25 each $3.00 p.doz.

891 Des. P.   891 Des. A.
MATCH HOLDER (4"x11')
Price $0.30 each
" 3.50 p.doz.

789 Des. K.   789 Des. M.
MATCH HOLDER (4"x 9")
Price $0.25 each $3.00 p.doz.

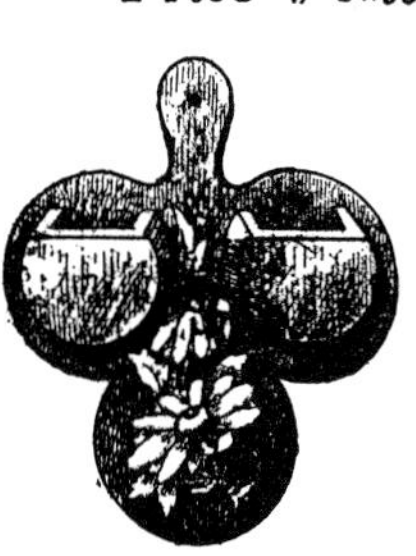

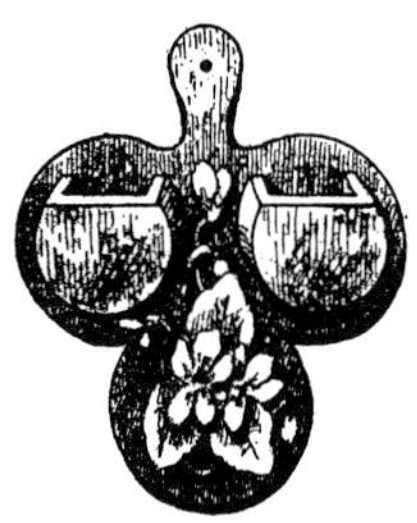

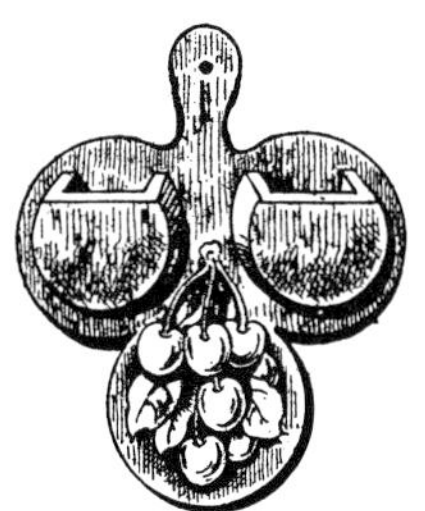

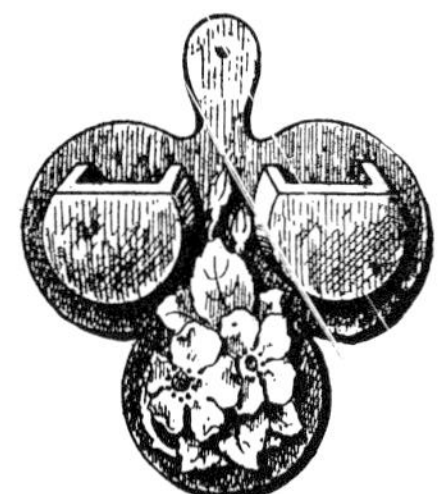

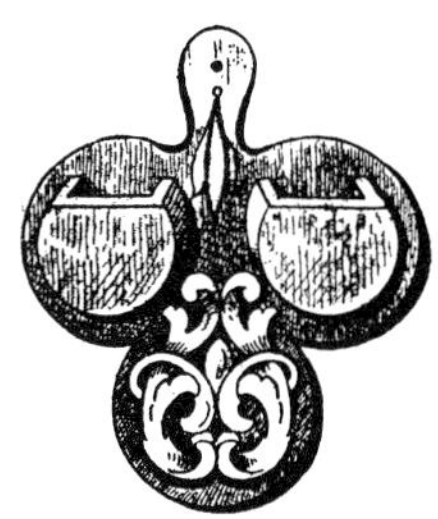

576 Des. N.   576 Des. H.   576 Des. M.   576 Des. E.   576 Des. G.

MATCH HOLDER (5⅜"x 6⅜") Price $0.25 each $3.00 p.doz.

722 Des. B. 4" diam

722 Des. A.

722 Des. C.

722 Des. J

PIN TRAY   (4" diam.)   Price $ 0.20 each $ 2.00 p.doz.

722 Des. M.

722 Des. G. 4" diam.

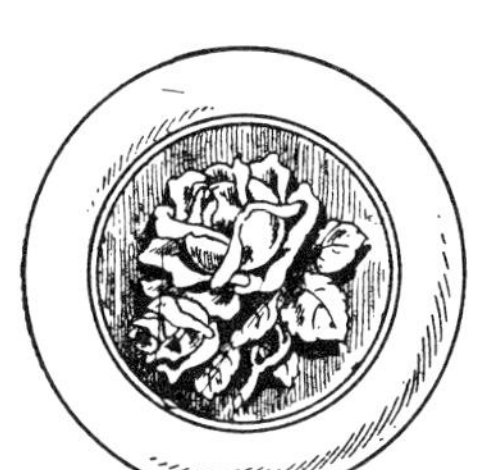

666 Des. C

713 Des. P.   (18" x 18")   CHECKER BOARD   Pr. $ 0.70 each   " 8.00 p.doz.

666 Des. L.

666 Des. J.
CARD RECEIVER   6" diam.
Price $ 0.30 each
" 3.60 p.doz.

666 Des. E.
CARD RECEIVER   6" diam
Price $ 0.30 each
" 3.60 p.doz.

712 Des. G.
FOLDING CHECKER BOARD

712 (open)   15" X 15"
Price $ 1.00 each
" 12.00 p.doz.

712 Des. B.
FOLDING CHECKER BOARD

655 Des. D. (7¾"×10")   655 Des. L. (7¾"×10")
CLOCK STAND without works Pr. $ 0.75 each $ 8.40 p.doz.
with works " $ 2.00 " $ 24.00

687 Des. Z. (9"×12")   687 Des. X. (9"×12")
CLOCK STAND without works Pr. $ 0.70 each $ 8.40 p.doz.
with works " $ 2.00 " $ 24.00 "

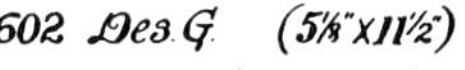

601 Des. A. (4¾"×14") 601 Des. G (4¾"×14") 601 Des. B.
CLOCK STAND without works Pr. $ 0.70 each $8.00 p.doz.
with works " $ 2.00 " $23.60 "

602 Des. G. (5½"×11½") 602 Des. M (5½"×11½") 602 Des. H.
CLOCK STAND without works Pr. $ 0.50 each $ 6.00 p.doz.
with works · $1.80 · $ 21.60 ·

715 Des. R. (5½"×10½") 715 Des. Q (5½"×10½") 715 Des. J (5½"×10½") 715 Des. G.
ALARM CLOCK STAND without works Pr. $ 0.70 each $ 8.40 p.doz.
with works $ 2.00 " $ 24.00 "

586   Des A.
586   Des B.
586   (French plate glass) 4½ inch   Des L
MIRROR Price $ 0.70 each " 8.00 p.doz.
586   (French plate glass) 4½ inch   Des C
MIRROR Price $ 0.70 each " 8.00 p.doz
586   Des H.
589   Des J.
589   Des K.L.
589   Des T.R.   (French plate glass 4½ inch)
589   Des K.R.
589   Des M.
MIRROR Price $ 0.70 each $ 8.00 p.doz
708   Des F.H.
708   Des J.N.
708   Des G. (6 inch French plate glass)
MIRROR Pr. $ 1.00 each $12.00 p.doz.
540   Des C.
540 Des F.H. (French plate glass 6 inch) MIRROR Price $ 1.00 each 12.00 p.doz.
540   Des B.
708   Des G.G. (French plate glass 6 inch)
MIRROR Pr. $ 1.00 each $12.00 p.doz.

551 Des. A.   551 Des. G.   551 Des. B.   551 Des. K.   551 Des. J.

THERMOMETER   (7" X 16½")   Price $ 0.80 each $ 9.60 p.doz.

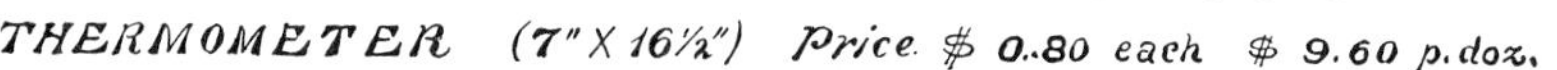

791 Des. C.
CALENDAR (5½" X 9½")
Price $ 0.25 each $ 3.⁰⁰ p.doz.

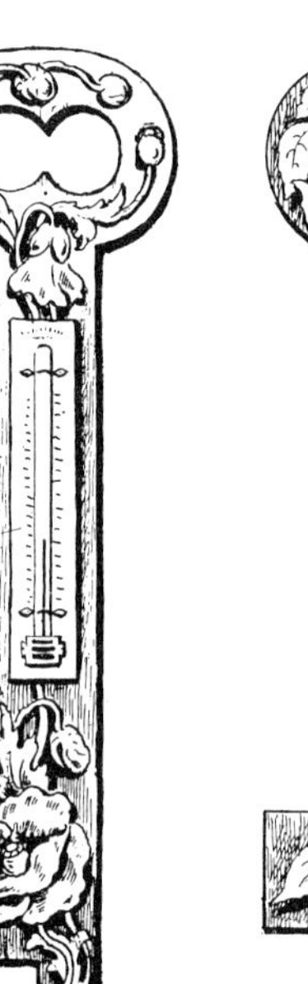
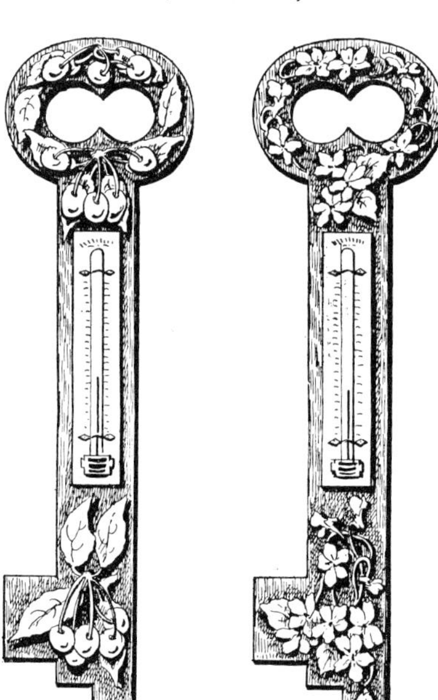

791 Des. A.
CALENDAR (5½" X 9½")
Price $ 0.25 each $ 3.⁰⁰ p.doz.

791 Des. G. (5½" X 9½")
CALENDAR   Price $ 0.25 each
" 3.⁰⁰ p.doz.

553 Des. B.   553 Des. M.   553 Des. H.

THERMOMETER   (4½" X 15¼")   Pr. $ 0.60 each $ 7.20 p.doz.

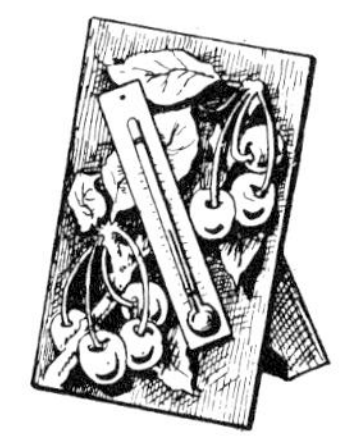

1005 Des. H.   1005 Des. N.   1005 Des. M.

THERMOMETER (3¼" X 5¼")   Price $ 0.25 each
" 2.50 p.doz.

791 Des. L. (5½" X 9½")
CALENDAR   Price $ 0.25 each
$ 3.⁰⁰ p.doz.

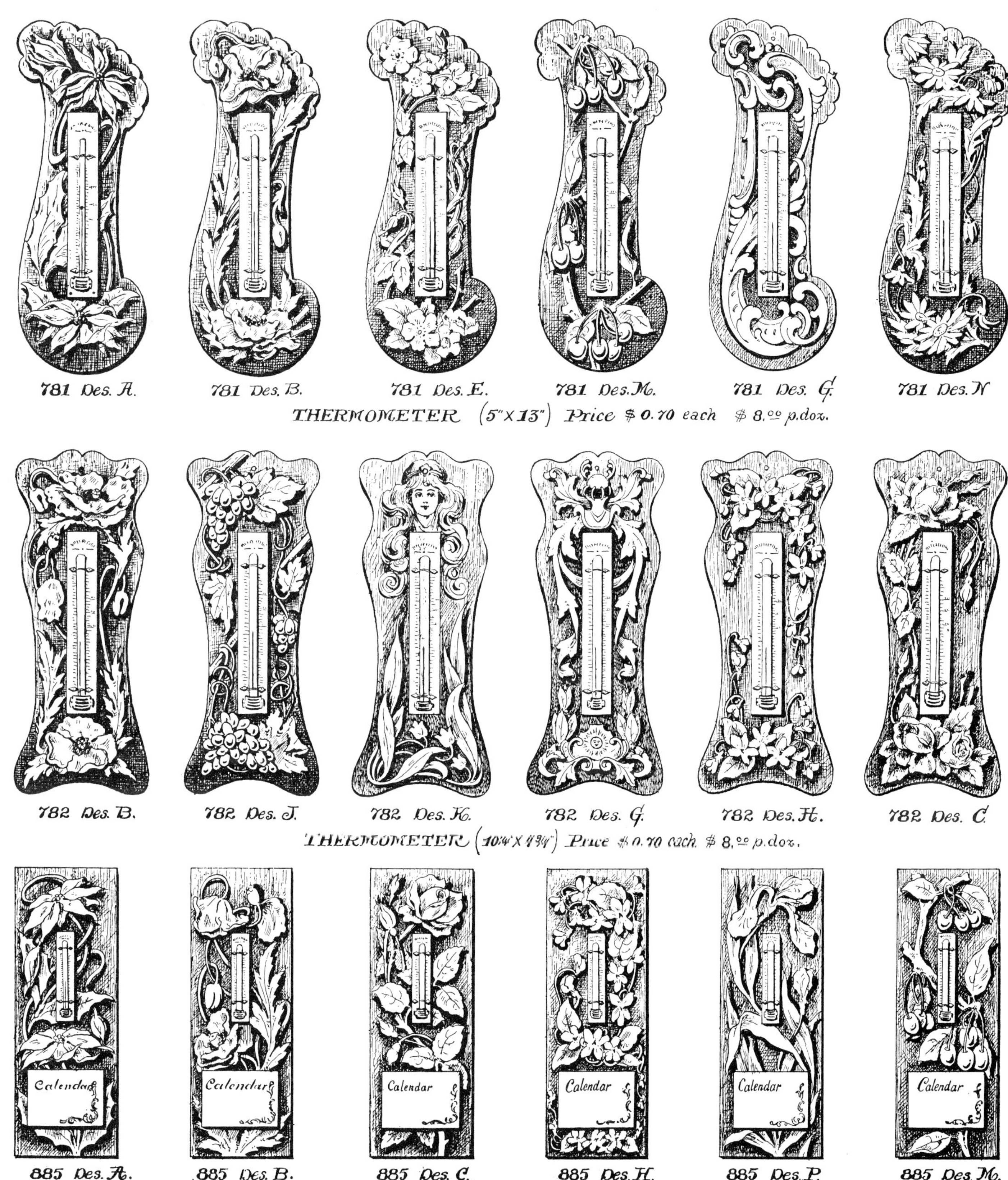

781 Des. A.
781 Des. B.
781 Des. E.
781 Des. M.
781 Des. G.
781 Des. N.
THERMOMETER (5"×13") Price $0.70 each $8.00 p.doz.
782 Des. B.
782 Des. J.
782 Des. K.
782 Des. G.
782 Des. H.
782 Des. C.
THERMOMETER (10¼"×4¾") Price $0.70 each $8.00 p.doz.
885 Des. A.
885 Des. B.
885 Des. C.
885 Des. H.
885 Des. P.
885 Des. M.
Calendar
Calendar
Calendar
Calendar
Calendar
Calendar
CALENDAR WITH THERMOMETER (4"×11") Price $0.35 each $4.00 p.doz.

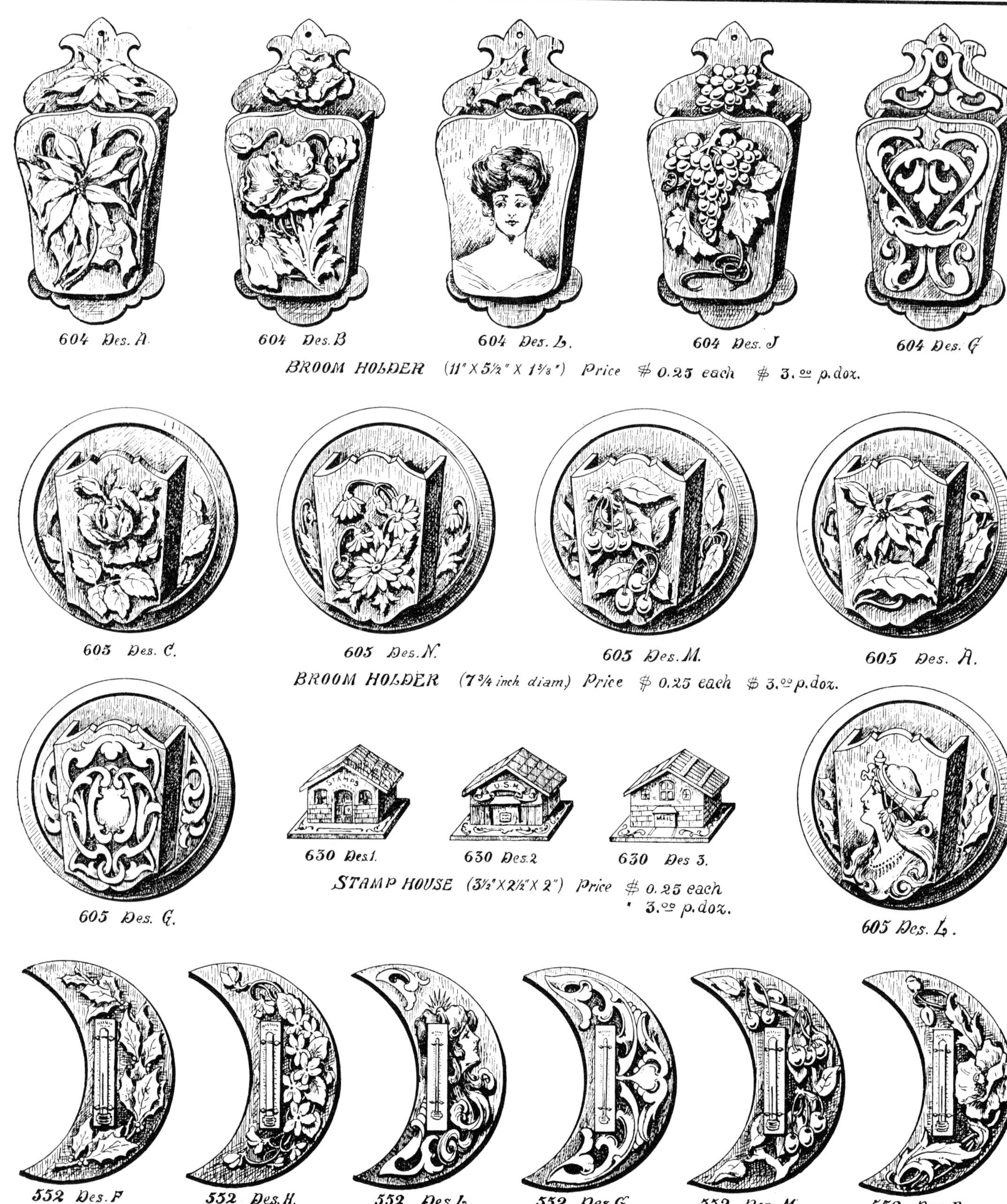

BROOM HOLDER (11" X 5½" X 1⅝") Price $ 0.25 each $ 3.⁰⁰ p. doz.

BROOM HOLDER (7¾ inch diam) Price $ 0.25 each $ 3.⁰⁰ p. doz.

STAMP HOUSE (3½" X 2½" X 2") Price $ 0.25 each ᐧ 3.⁰⁰ p. doz.

(8" X 5⅜") *CRESCENT THERMOMETER* Price $ 0.45 each $ 5.⁰⁰ p. doz.

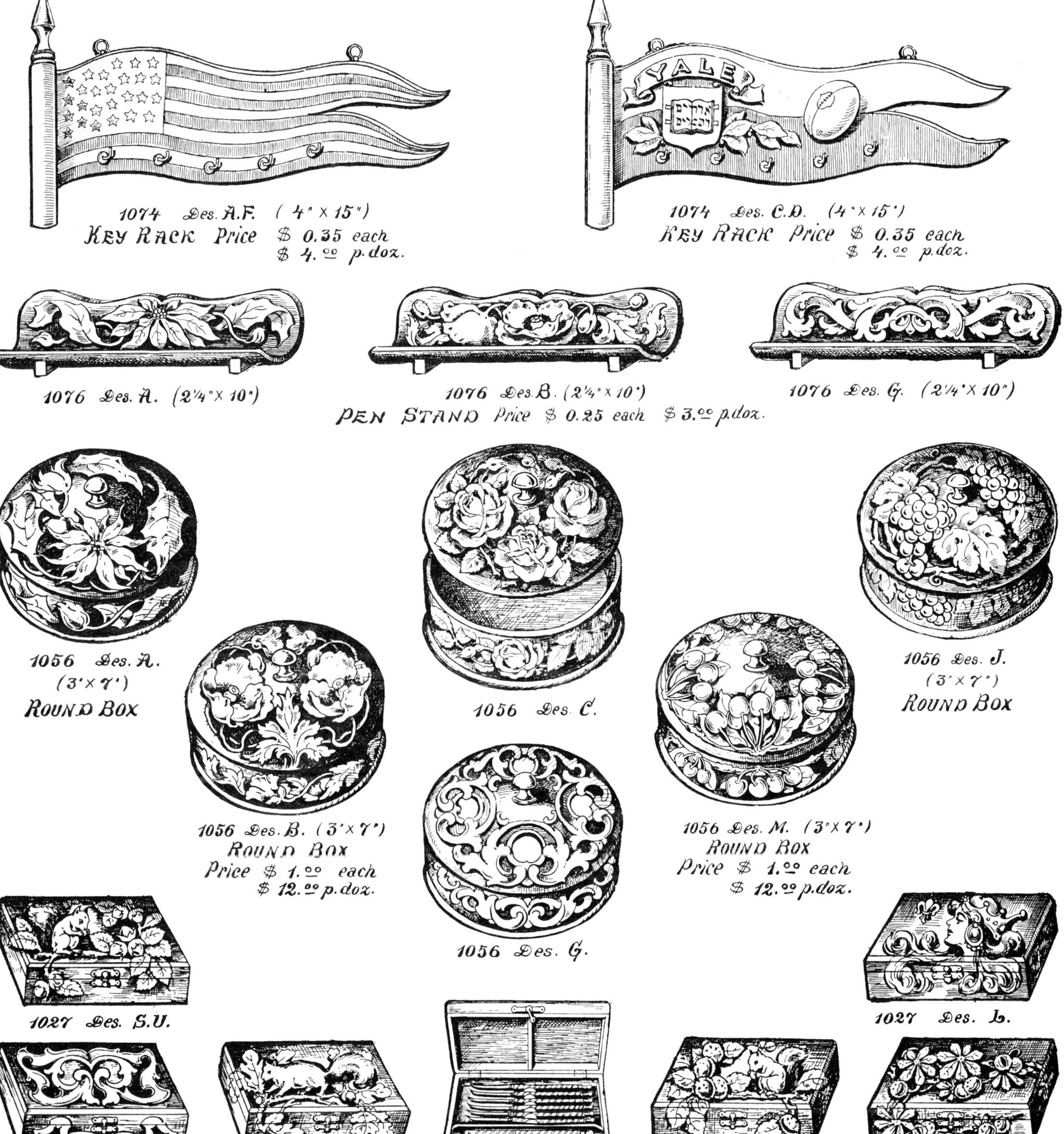

1074　Des. A.F.　(4" × 15")
KEY RACK Price　$ 0.35 each
$ 4.⁰⁰ p. doz.

1074　Des. C.D.　(4" × 15")
KEY RACK Price　$ 0.35 each
$ 4.⁰⁰ p. doz.

1076　Des. A.　(2¼" × 10")

1076　Des. B.　(2¼" × 10")
PEN STAND Price $ 0.25 each $ 3.⁰⁰ p. doz.

1076　Des. G.　(2¼" × 10")

1056　Des. A.
(3" × 7")
ROUND BOX

1056　Des. B.　(3" × 7")
ROUND BOX
Price $ 1.⁰⁰ each
$ 12.⁰⁰ p. doz.

1056　Des. C.

1056　Des. G.

1056　Des. M.　(3" × 7")
ROUND BOX
Price $ 1.⁰⁰ each
$ 12.⁰⁰ p. doz.

1056　Des. J.
(3" × 7")
ROUND BOX

1027　Des. S.U.

1027　Des. L.

1027　Des. G.　(1½" × 4½" × 6")

1027　Des. SS.

NUT PICK SET　INCL. 6 NUT PICKS & CRACKER
Price　$ 0.70 each　$ 8.⁰⁰ p. doz.

1027　Des. U.S.　(1½" × 4½" × 6")

1027　Des. U.

628 Des. A. (8"x9¾"x11¾")
MAGAZINE STAND   Pr. $0.75 each $9.00 p.doz.

777 Des. N.

777 Des. S.

628 Des. G. (8"x9¾"x11¾")
MAGAZINE STAND   Pr. $0.75 each $9.00 p.doz.

627 Des. B. (8"x9¾"x11¾")
MAGAZINE STAND   Pr. $0.75 each $9.00 p.doz.

777 Des. M.

777 Des. G.
STAMP BOX (2"x4½")
Price $0.35 each
" 4.00 p.doz.

627 Des. J. (8"x9¾"x11¾")
MAGAZINE STAND   Pr. $0.75 each $9.00 p.doz.

776 Des. N.

776 Des. E.

776 Des. G.

776 Des. H.
STAMP BOX (2"x3")
Price $0.25 each
" 3.00 p.doz.

956 Des. K. (6"x15½"x20½") *MEDICINE CABINET*
Price $4.00 each $48.00 p.doz.

957 Des. T.
CIGAR CABINET *Price* $4.00 each
(7"x13½"x20½") " 48.00 p.doz.

ASSORTED BRUSHES
FINEST QUALITY, SUPERB BRISTLES, WELL MADE AND DURABLE

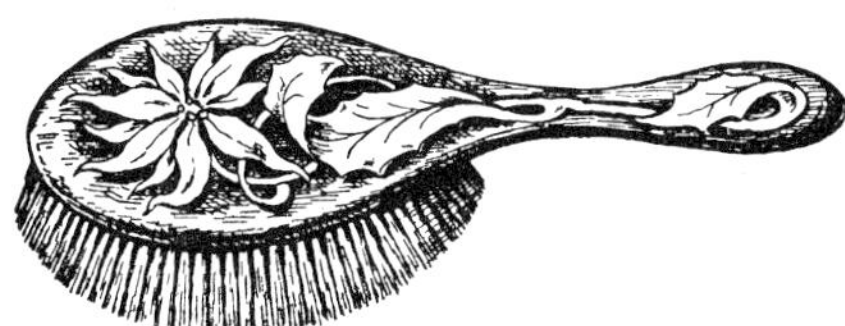

595 Des. A.
Hair Brush Pr. $ 1.35 each
" 16.00 p.doz.

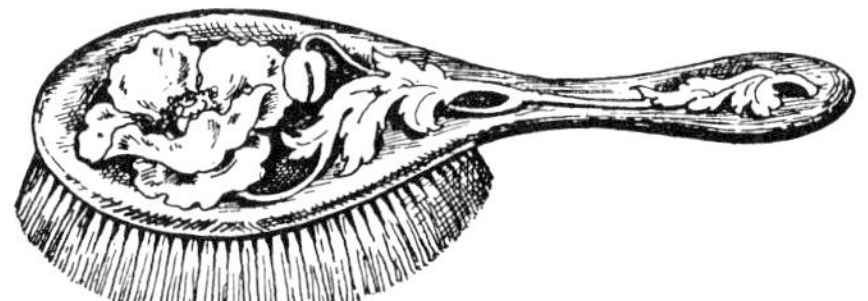

595 Des. B.
Hair Brush Pr. $ 1.35 each
" 16.00 p.doz.

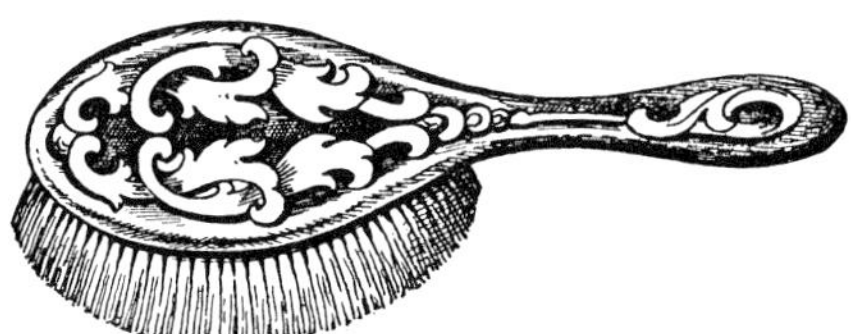

595 Des. G.
Hair Brush Pr. $ 1.35 each
" 16.00 p.doz.

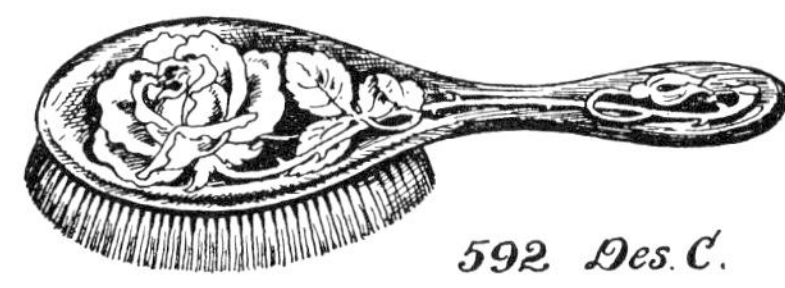

592 Des. C.
Hair Brush Pr. $ 1.00 each
" 12.00 p.doz.

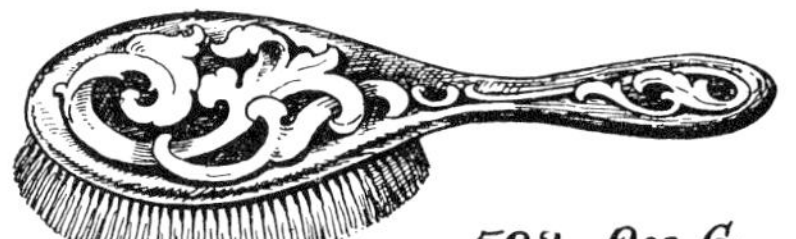

592 Des. G.
Hair Brush Pr. $ 1.00 each
" 12.00 p.doz.

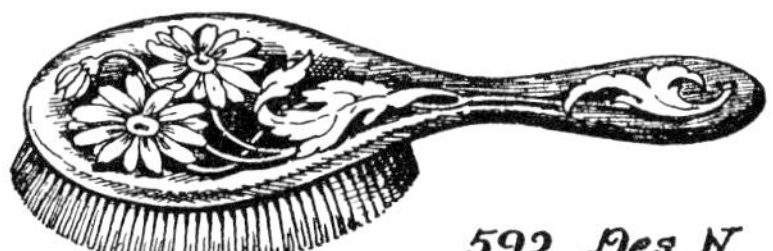

592 Des. N.
Hair Brush Pr. $ 1.00 each
" 12.00 p.doz.

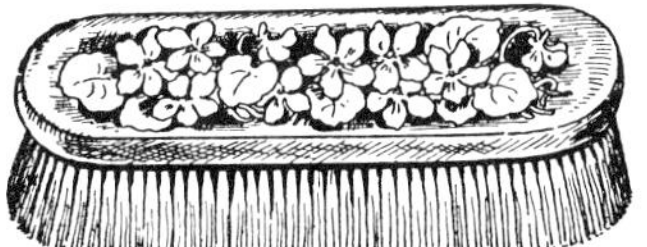

593 Des. H.

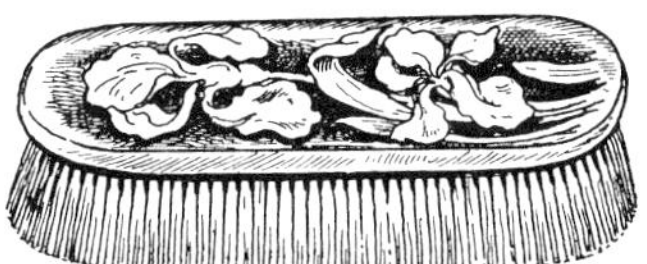

593 Des. P.
Cloth Brush Pr. $ 1.00 each
" 12.00 p.doz.

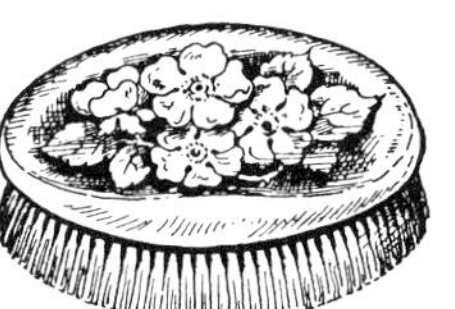

591 Des. E.

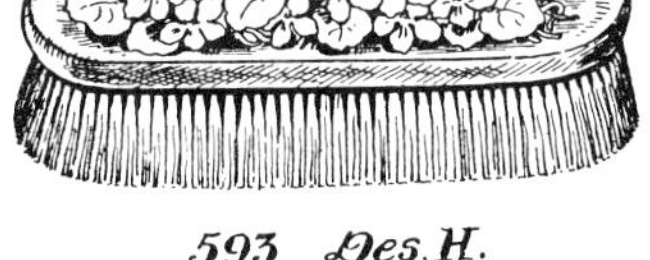

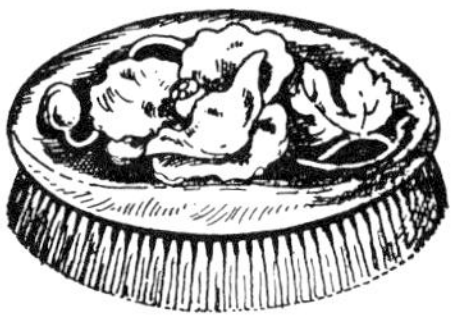

591 Des. B.
Military Brush Pr. $ 1.00 each
" 12.00 p.doz.

635 Des. F.

635 Des. D.
Hair Brush Price $ 0.60 each
" 7.20 p.doz.

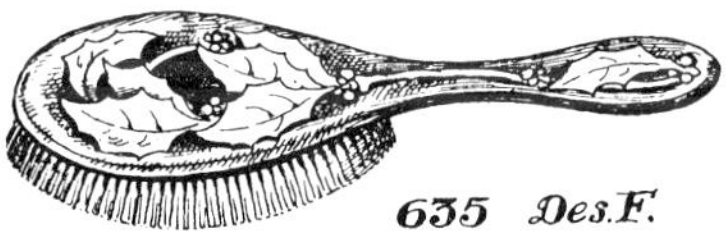

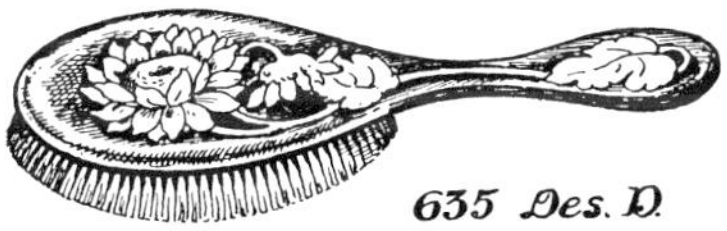

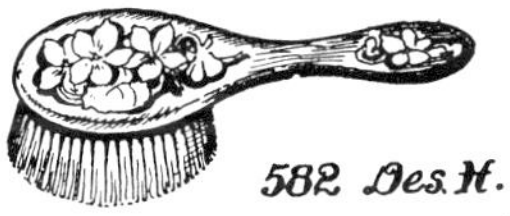

582 Des. H.

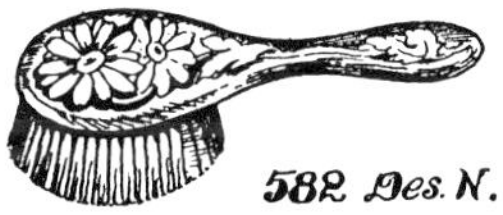

582 Des. N.
Baby Hair Brush Pr. $ 0.50 each
" 6.00 p.doz.

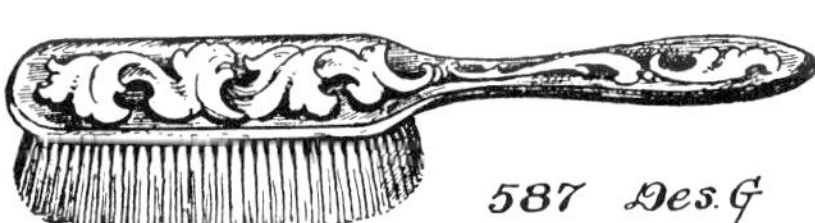

587 Des. G
Ladies Hat Brush Pr $ 0.60 each
" 7.20 p.doz.

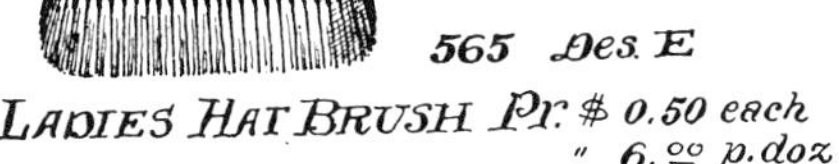

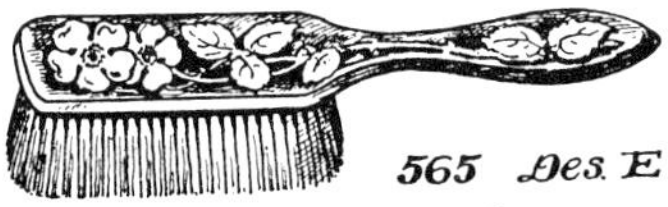

565 Des. E
Ladies Hat Brush Pr. $ 0.50 each
" 6.00 p.doz.

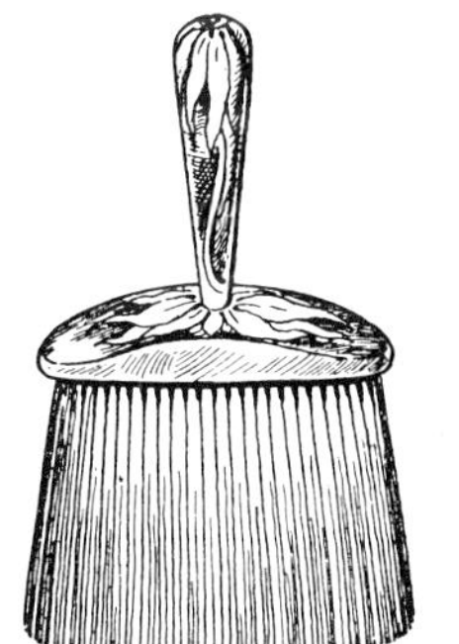

581 Des. A.
Bonnet Brush
Pr. $ 0.75 each $ 8.50 p.doz.

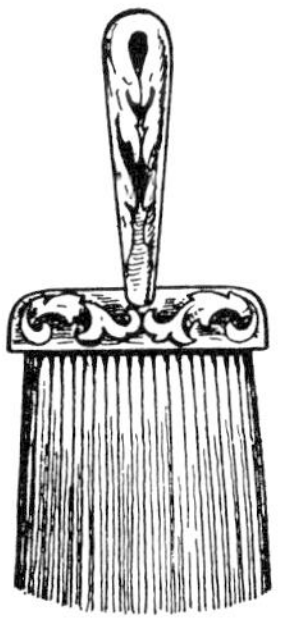

588 Des. G.
Bonnet Brush
Pr $ 0.60 each $ 7.20 p.doz.

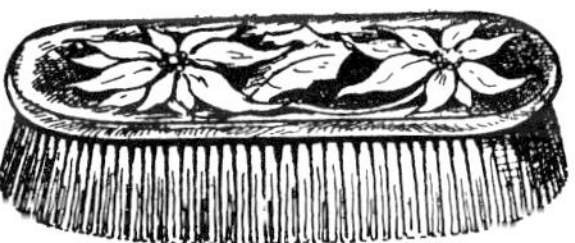

638 Des. A.
Cloth Brush Pr. $ 0.60 each
" 7.20 p.doz.

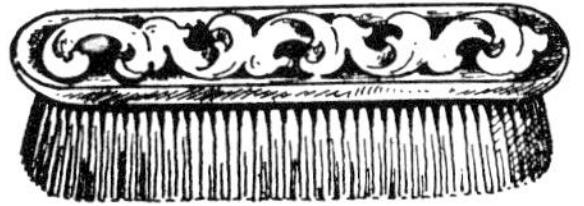

636 Des G.
Hat Brush Pr. $ 0.60 each
" 7.20 p.doz.

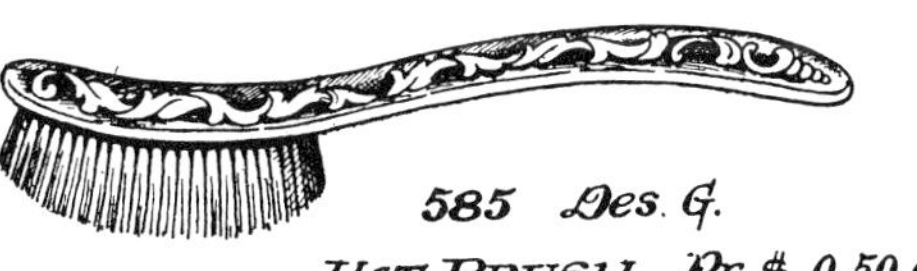

585 Des. G.
Hat Brush Pr. $ 0.50 each
" 6.00 p.doz.

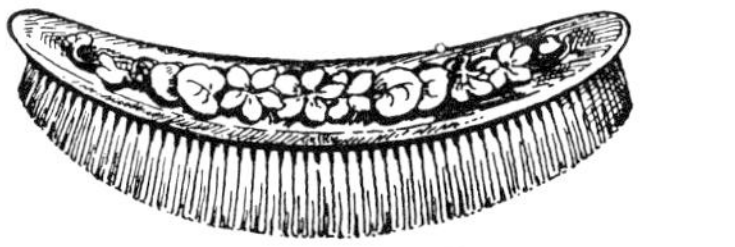

594 Des. H.
Crescent Hat Brush Pr. $ 0.60 each
" 7.20 p.doz.

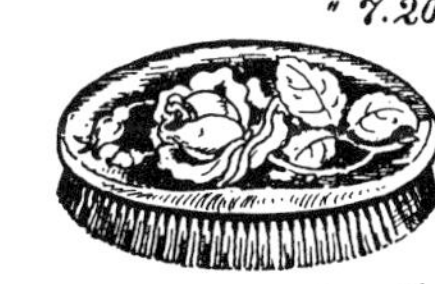

637 Des. C.
Military Brush
Pr. $ 0.60 each $ 7.20 p.doz.

898 *Des. M. (10" diam.)*
French Plate Glass 6 inch
WALL MIRROR Pr. $ 1.⁰⁰ each
" 12.⁰⁰ p. doz.

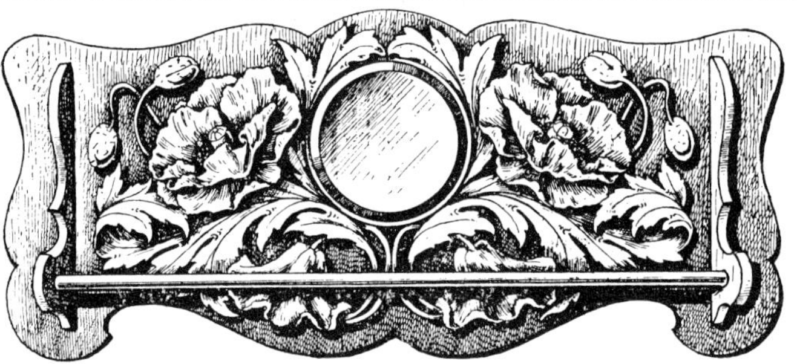

744 Des. B. (9"X21") TIE or TOWEL RACK Pr. $ 1.30 each
" 15.60 p. doz.

898 *Des. H. (10" diam.)*
French Plate Glass 6 inch
WALL MIRROR Pr. $ 1.⁰⁰ each
" 12.⁰⁰ p. doz.

744 Des. J. (9"X21") TIE or TOWEL RACK Pr. $ 1.30 each
" 15.60 p. doz.

898 *Des. A. (10" diam.)*
French Plate Glass 6 inch
WALL MIRROR Pr. $ 1.⁰⁰ each
" 12.⁰⁰ p. doz.

898 *Des. G. (10" diam)*
French Plate Glass 6 inch
WALL MIRROR Pr. $ 1.⁰⁰ each
" 12.⁰⁰ p. doz.

744 Des. G. (9"X21") TIE or TOWEL RACK Pr. $ 1.30 each
" 15.60 p. doz.

743 Des. L. (9"X21") TIE or TOWEL RACK Pr. $ 0.50 each
" 6.⁰⁰ p. doz.

743 Des. O. (9"X21") TIE or TOWEL RACK Pr. $ 0.50 each
" 6.⁰⁰ p. doz.

743 Des. C. (9"X21") TIE or TOWEL RACK Pr. $ 0.50 each
" 6.⁰⁰ p. doz.

743 Des. B. 9"X21" TIE or TOWEL RACK Pr. $ 0.50 each
" 6.⁰⁰ p. doz.

1007 Des. A. (5¾" × 17¼") TIE RACK.

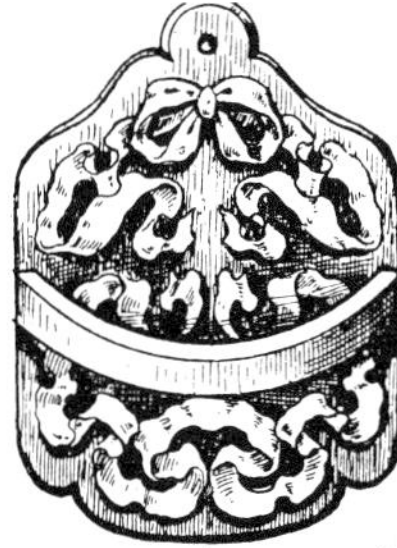

718 Des. G. (6"×8")

1007 Des. B. (5¾"×17¼") TIE RACK

1007 Des. L. (5¾"×17¼") TIE RACK
Price $ 0.50 each $ 6.⁰⁰ p.doz.

718 Des. C. (6"×8")
TIE RACK. Pr. $ 0.25 each $ 3.⁰⁰ p.doz

1007 Des. J. (5¾"×17¼") TIE RACK.
Price $ 0.50 each $ 6.⁰⁰ p.doz.

1021 Des. J.N. (8½"×20") TIE RACK
Price $ 0.75 each $ 9.⁰⁰ p.doz.

981
PAPER CUTTER
Pr. $ 0.25 each $ 2.50 p.doz.

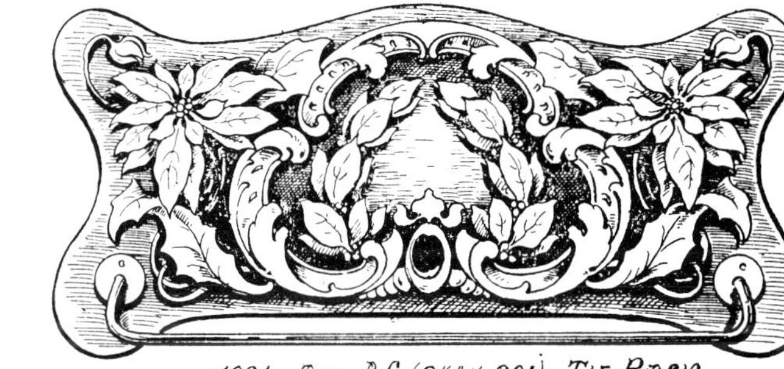

1021 Des. A.G. (8½"×20") TIE RACK
Price $ 0.75 each $ 9.⁰⁰ p.doz.

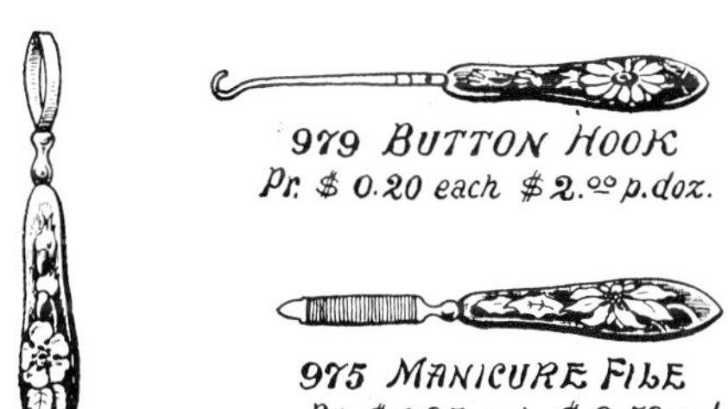

979 BUTTON HOOK
Pr. $ 0.20 each $ 2.⁰⁰ p.doz.

975 MANICURE FILE
Pr. $ 0.25 each $ 2.50 p.doz.

978
TWEETZERS
Pr. $ 0.25 each
$ 2.50 p.doz.

980
SHOE HORN
Pr. $ 0.20 each
$ 2.⁰⁰ p.doz.

977
CORN KNIFE
Pr. $ 0.25 each $ 2.50 p.doz.

974 HAIR CURLER
Pr. $ 0.25 each $ 2.50 p.doz.

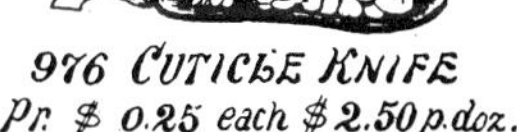

976 CUTICLE KNIFE
Pr. $ 0.25 each $ 2.50 p.doz.

982
INK ERASER
Pr. $ 0.25 each $ 2.50 p.doz.

984
GLOVE STRETCHER
Pr. $ 1.⁰⁰ each
$ 12.⁰⁰ p.doz.

983
MONOGRAM SEAL
Pr. $ 0.25 each $ 2.50 p.doz.

842 Des. A. 842 Des. B. 842 Des. C. 842 Des. G.
NAPKIN RING Price $ 0.20 each $ 2.⁰⁰ p.doz.

742 Des. F.H. (11½"×18") MUSIC RACK
Price $ 1.35 each $ 15.60 p.doz.

843 Des. E. 843 Des. M. 843 Des. N. 843 Des. J.
NAPKIN RING Price $ 0.20 each $ 2.⁰⁰ p.doz.

703 Des. A. (3¾" × 8")

703 Des. B. (3¾" × 8")
LETTER RACK

703 Des. C. (3¾" × 8")
Price $ 0.30 each
" 3.50 p. doz.

703 Des. M. (3¾" × 8")

703 Des. K. (3¾" × 8")

703 Des. G (3¾" × 8")

625 Des. L. (9½" × 7" × 3⅛")
STATIONERY RACK Pr. $ 0.40 each
" 4.50 p. doz.

811 Des. N.   811 Des. H.
CARD STAND (6" × 5" × 2½")
Price $ 0.35 each
" 4.00 p. doz.

625 Des. G. (9½" × 7" × 3⅛")
STATIONERY RACK Pr. $ 0.40 each
" 4.50 p. doz.

625 Des. J. (9½" × 7" × 3¼")
STATIONERY RACK Pr. $ 0.40 each
" 4.50 p. doz.

811 Des. M.   811 Des. E.
CARD STAND (6" × 5" × 2½")
Price $ 0.35 each
" 4.00 p. doz.

625 Des. B. (9½" × 7" × 3⅛")
STATIONERY RACK Pr. $ 0.40 each
" 4.50 p. doz.

625 Des. P. (9½" × 7" × 3¼")
STATIONERY RACK Pr. $ 0.40 each
" 4.50 p. doz.

811 Des. F.   811 Des. G.
CARD STAND (6" × 5" × 2½")
Price $ 0.35 each
" 4.00 p. doz.

625 Des. C. (9½" × 7" × 3¼")
STATIONERY RACK Pr. $ 0.40 each
" 4.50 p. doz.

WASTE BASKETS

641   Des. R.

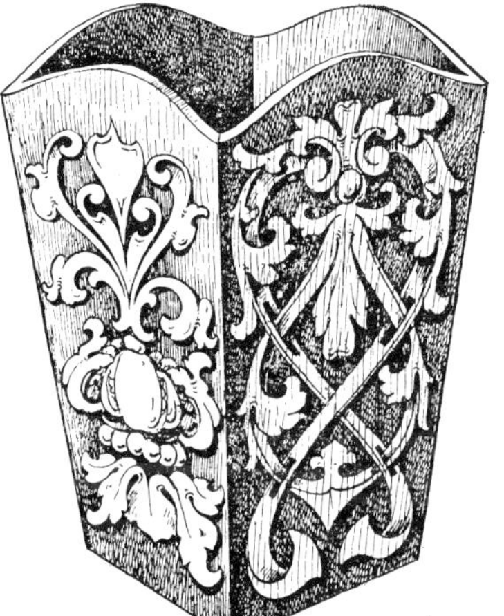

641   Des. B.

643 Des. G.
(9½" × 18")

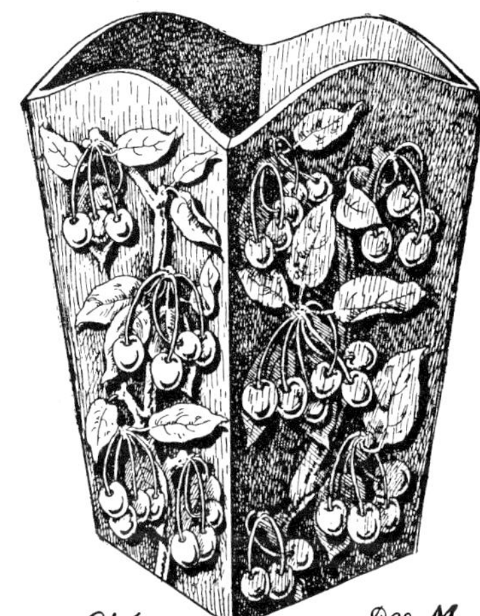

641   Des. M.
WASTE BASKET (8½" × 13¾")
(knocked down) Pr. $ 0.70 each $ 8.00 p.doz.

641   Des. G.
WASTE BASKET (8½" × 13¾")
(knocked down) Pr. $ 0.70 each $ 8.00 p.doz.

643 Des. K. (9½" × 18")
WASTE BASKET (knocked down.)

Price $ 1.25 each $ 14.40 p.doz.

643   Des. J.

643   Des. A.

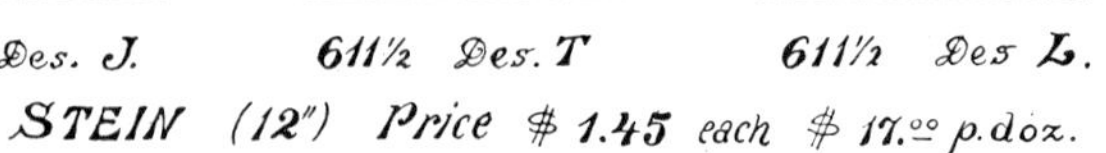

611½ Des. J.   611½ Des. T   611½ Des. L.   612 Des. J.   612 Des. T   612 Des. G.

STEIN (12") Price $ 1.45 each $ 17.00 p. doz.   STEIN (9") Price $ 1.25 each
" 14.40 p. doz.

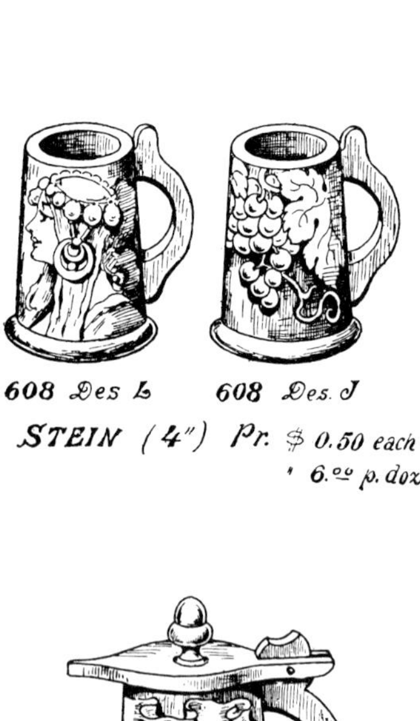

608 Des. L   608 Des. J

STEIN (4") Pr. $ 0.50 each
" 6.00 p. doz.

609 Des. G.   609 Des. T.

STEIN (6") Pr. $ 0.70 each
" 8.00 p. doz.

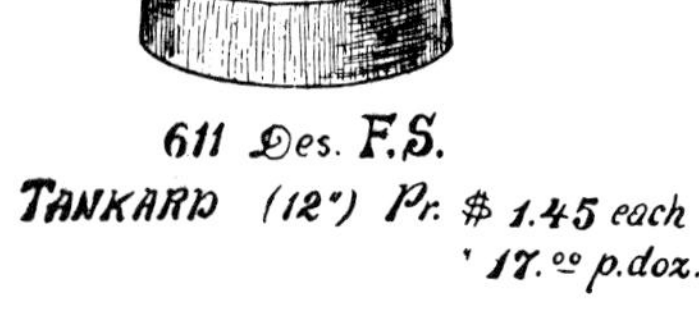

611 Des. F.S.   610 Des. J.   610 Des. T.   611 Des. T.

TANKARD (12") Pr. $ 1.45 each   TANKARD (22") Price $ 2.50 each   TANKARD (12") Pr. $ 1.45 each
" 17.00 p. doz.   " 30.00 p. doz.   " 17.00 p. doz.

735 Des. T. (11"x19½")
STEIN RACK AND SHELF Price $ 1.35 each
" 15.60 p. doz.

736 Des. J. (14"x16")
STEIN RACK AND SHELF
Price $ 1.35 each
" 15.60 p. doz.

737 Des. T. (15"x21")
STEIN RACK AND SHELF Price $ 1.80 each
" 21.60 p. doz.

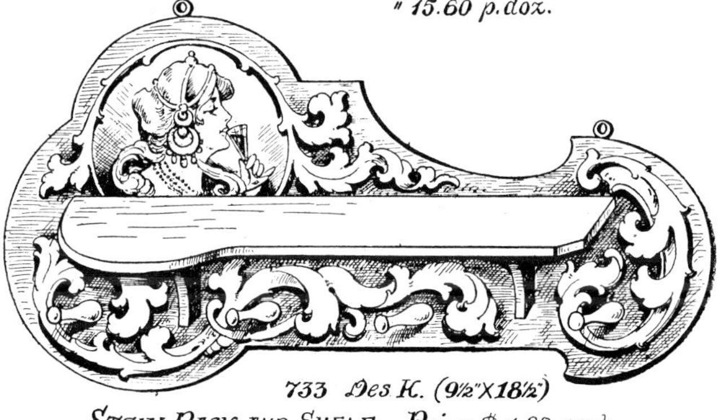

733 Des. K. (9½"x18½")
STEIN RACK AND SHELF Price $ 1.00 each
" 12.00 p. doz.

734 Des. G. STEIN RACK & SHELF (8"x21½") Pr. $ 1.00 each
" 12.00 p. doz.

741 Des. A. (12"x15½")
PAPER RACK Price $ 1.35 each
$ 15.60 p. doz.

1028 Des. M.   (12½" diam.)
COCKTAIL TRAY (Fitted with glass)
Price $ 1.35 each $ 16.⁰⁰ p. doz.

1028 Des. G.   (12" diam.)

1028 Des. B.   (12½" diam.)
COCKTAIL TRAY (Fitted with glass)
Price $ 1.35 each $ 16.⁰⁰ p. doz.

797 Des. A. (7¾"×12¾") TRAY Pr. $ 1.⁰⁰ each
" 12.⁰⁰ p. doz.

812 Des. B. (3"×7")

812 Des. M. (3"×7")
TRAY
Price $ 0.25 each
" 3.⁰⁰ p. doz.

797 Des. M. (7¾"×12¾") TRAY Pr. $ 1.⁰⁰ each
" 12.⁰⁰ p. doz.

798 Des. J. (9½"×15½") TRAY Pr. $ 1.20 each
" 14.40 p. doz.

798 Des. G. (9½"×15½") TRAY Pr. $ 1.20 each
" 14.40 p. doz.

799 Des. G. (11½"×18") TRAY Pr. $ 1.35 each
" 16.⁰⁰ p. doz.

799 Des. B. (11½"×18") TRAY Pr. $ 1.35 each
" 16.⁰⁰ p. doz.

1028 Des. A.R. (12½" diam.)
COCKTAIL TRAY (Fitted with glass)
Price $1.35 each $16.00 p. doz.

1028 Des. V. (12½" diam.)

1028 Des. M.R. (12½" diam.)
COCKTAIL TRAY (Fitted with glass)
Price $1.35 each $16.00 p. doz.

794 Des. M. (7½ X 12") TRAY Pr. $0.85 each
" 10.00 p. doz.

812 Des. N. (3" X 7")

812 Des. G. (3" X 7")
PEN TRAY
Price $0.25 each
" 3.00 p. doz.

794 Des. B. (7½ X 12") TRAY Pr. $0.85 each
" 10.00 p. doz.

795 Des. A. (9" X 15") TRAY Pr. $1.00 each
" 12.00 p. doz.

795 Des. J. (9" X 15") TRAY Pr. $1.00 each
" 12.00 p. doz.

796 Des. G. (10½" X 18") TRAY Pr. $1.20 each
" 14.00 p. doz.

796 Des. M.M. (10½" X 18") TRAY Pr. $1.20 each
" 14.00 p. doz.

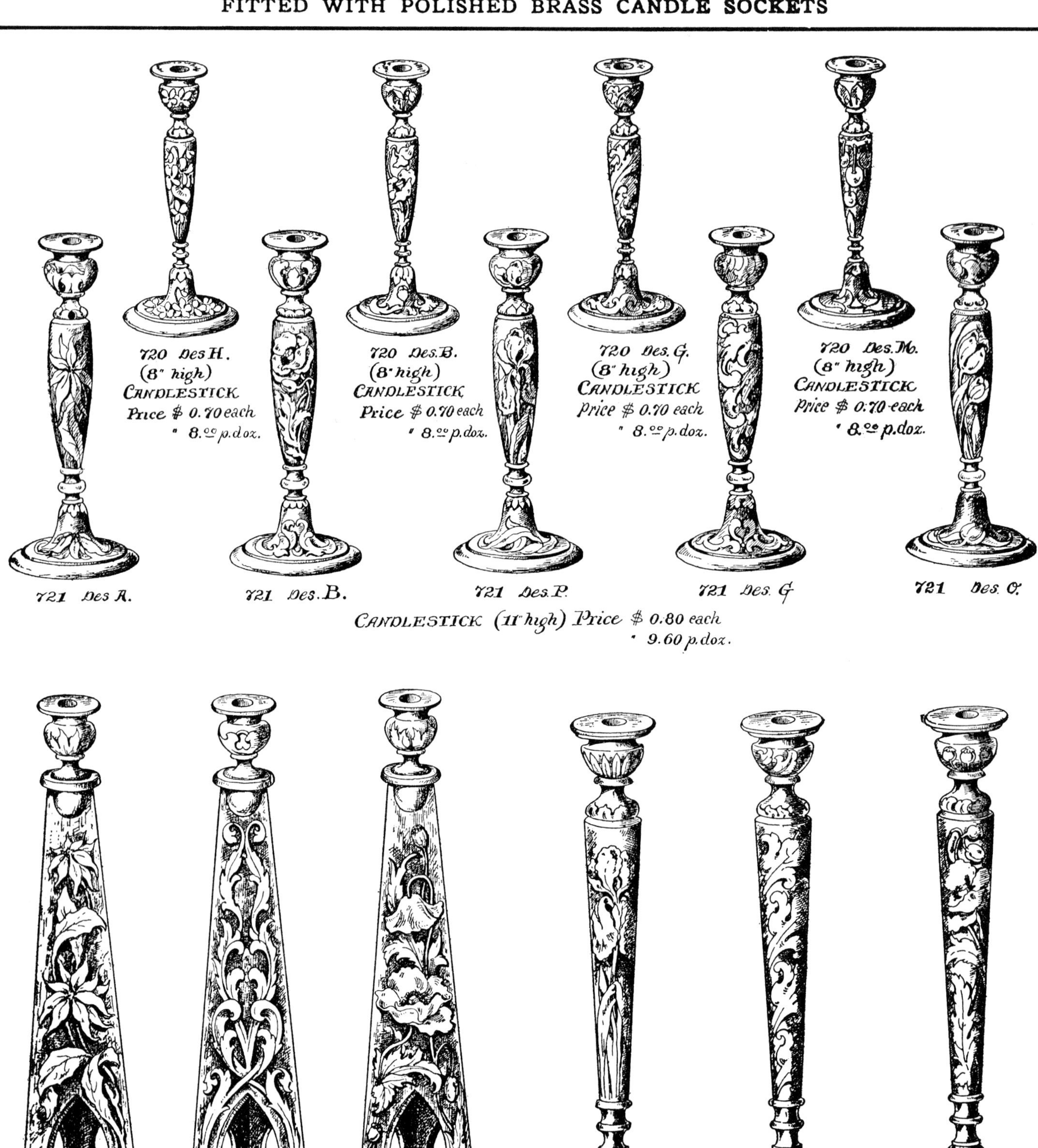
720 Des H.
(8" high)
CANDLESTICK
Price $ 0.70 each
" 8.00 p.doz.

720 Des B.
(8" high)
CANDLESTICK
Price $ 0.70 each
" 8.00 p.doz.

720 Des. G.
(8" high)
CANDLESTICK
Price $ 0.70 each
" 8.00 p.doz.

720 Des. M.
(8" high)
CANDLESTICK
Price $ 0.70 each
" 8.00 p.doz.

721 Des A.   721 Des. B.   721 Des. P.   721 Des. G.   721 Des. O.

CANDLESTICK (11" high) Price $ 0.80 each
" 9.60 p.doz.

973 Des. A.   973 Des. G.   973 Des B.   719 Des. P.   719 Des. G.   719 Des. B.
CANDLESTICK (5"x20") Price $ 1.00 each   CANDLESTICK (18" high) Price $ 1.00 each
" 12.00 p.doz   " 12.00 p.doz.

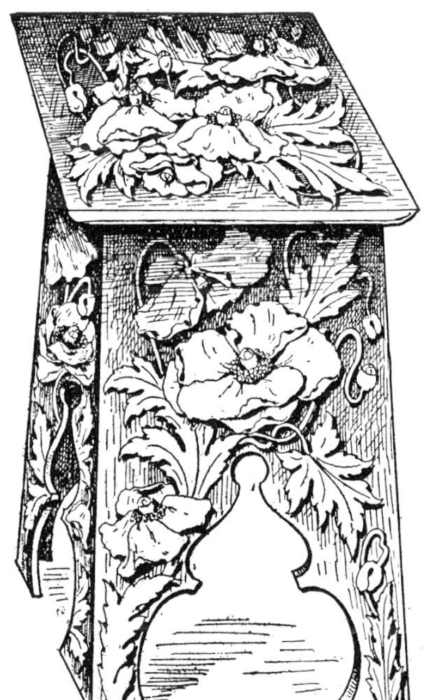

ALL TABOURETTES MADE WITH 3-PLY TOPS. SUITABLE FOR CARVING AND DEEP BURNING, WITH BEAUTIFUL RESULTS

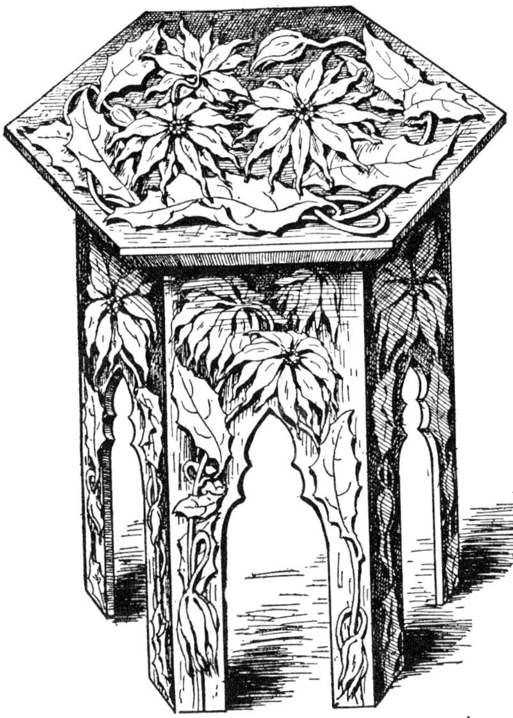

645. Des. A. (17¾" X 21")
Price $ 4.00 each
" 48.00 p.doz.

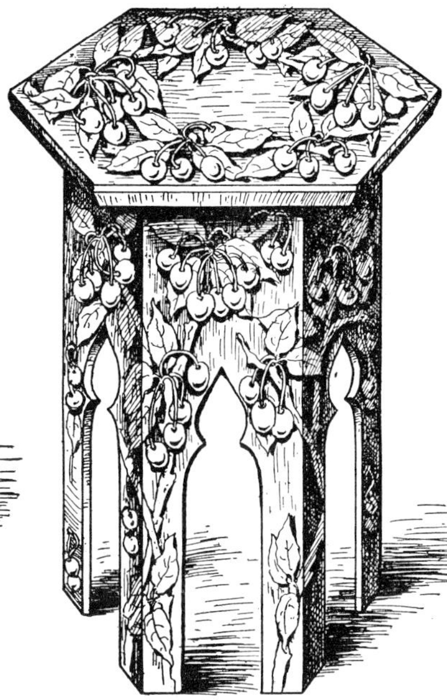

644 Des M. (15" x 21")
Price $ 2.25 each
" 27 00 p.doz.

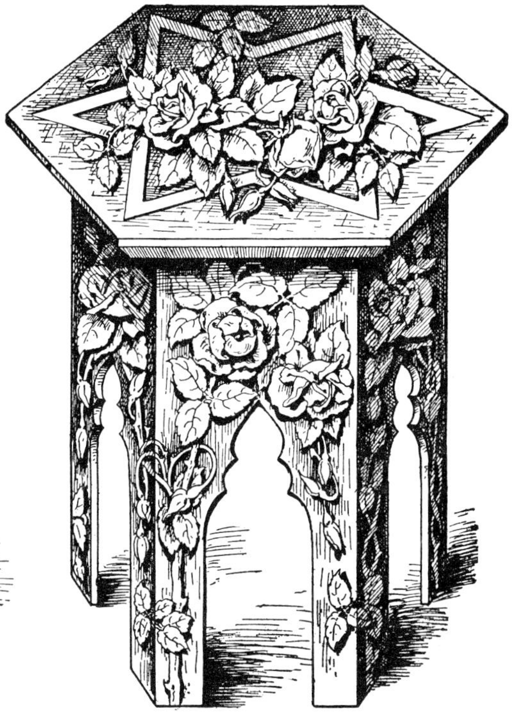

645 Des C. (17¾" X 21")
Price $ 4.00 each
" 48 00 p.doz.

648 Des. B. (14" X 21")
Price $ 4.00 each
" 48.00 p.doz.

645 Des G. (17¾" X 21")
Price $ 4.00 each
" 48.00 p.doz.

648 Des J. (14" X 21")
Price $ 4.00 each
" 48.00 p.doz.

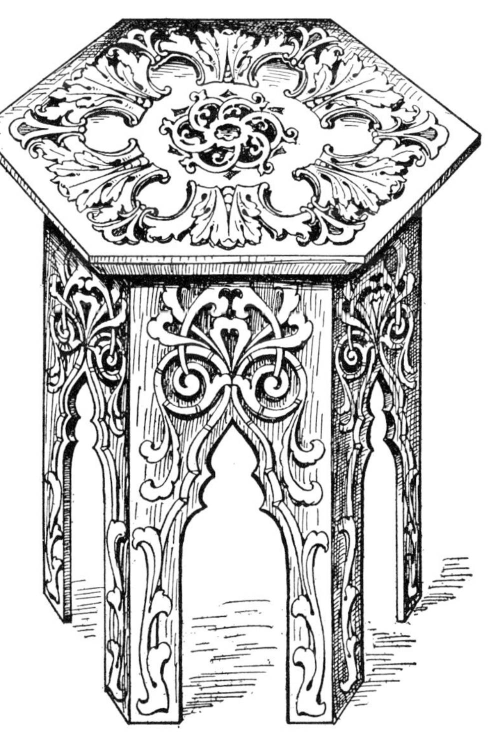

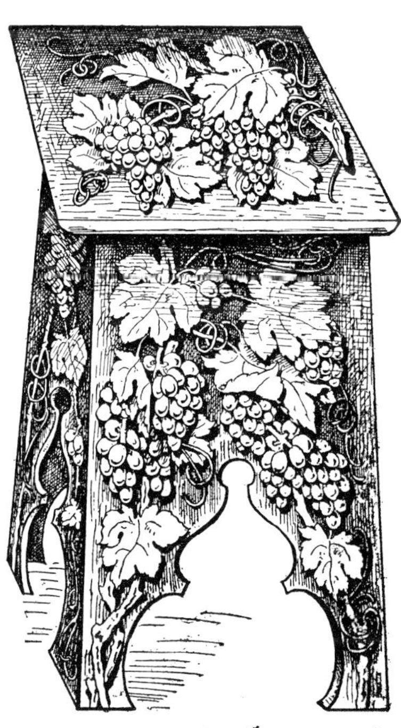

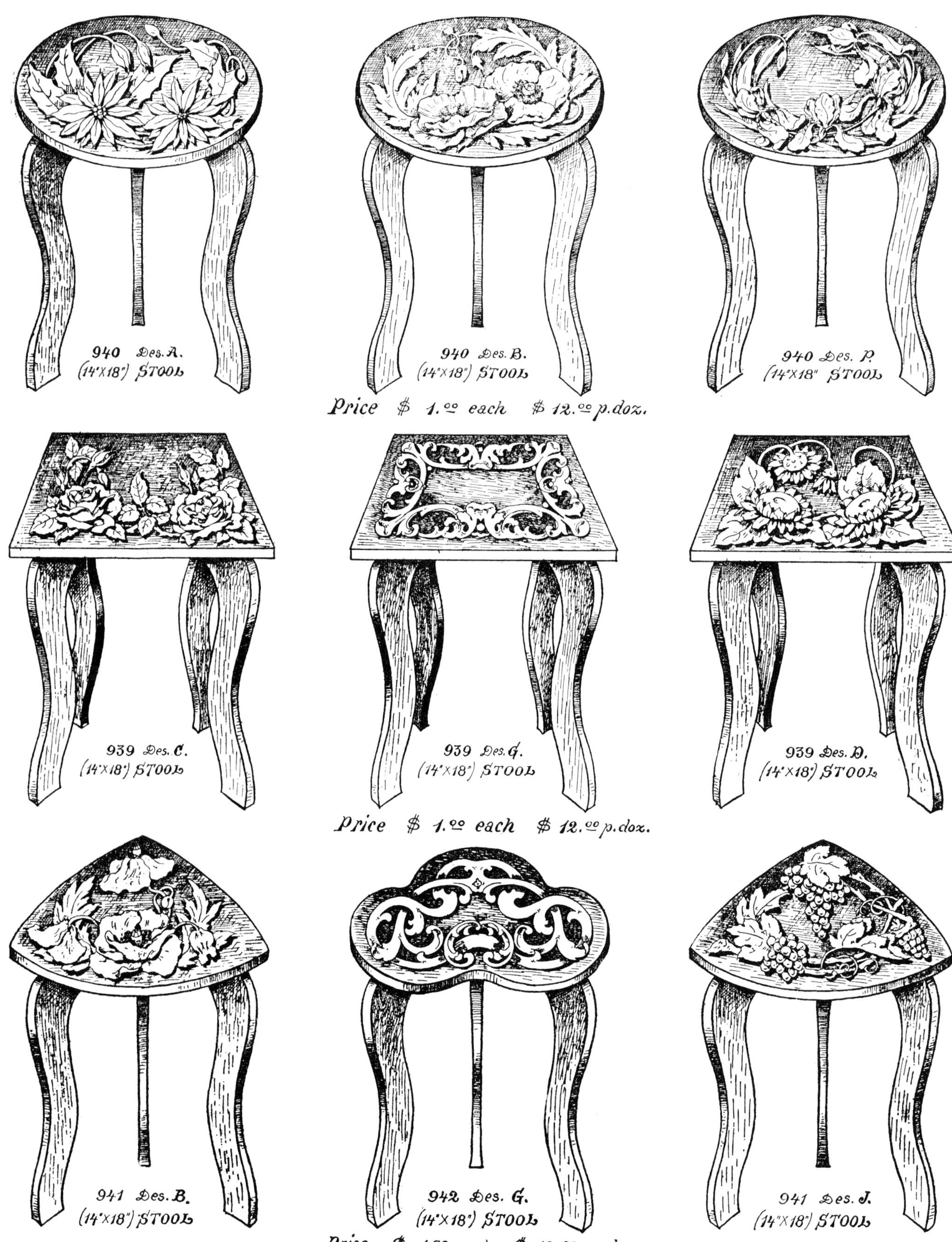

940 Des. A.
(14"x18") STOOL
940 Des. B.
(14"x18") STOOL
940 Des. P.
(14"x18") STOOL
Price $ 1.00 each $ 12.00 p.doz.
939 Des. C.
(14"x18") STOOL
939 Des. G.
(14"x18") STOOL
939 Des. D.
(14"x18") STOOL
Price $ 1.00 each $ 12.00 p.doz.
941 Des. B.
(14"x18") STOOL
942 Des. G.
(14"x18") STOOL
941 Des. J.
(14"x18") STOOL
Price $ 1.00 each $ 12.00 p.doz.

921.
29' × 18 inch
Cellarette.
Each $6.00; Doz., $72.00
922.
30' × 28 inch
Combination Chair
and Table.
Price, Each $8.00; Doz., $96.00
937.
15' × 8½ inch
Foot Stool   (Folding)
Each $1.35; Doz., $16.00
907.
20' × 17 inch
Bench.
Price, Each $4.00;
Doz., $48.00
906.   31" × 22 inch
Library Chair.
Price, Each $7.00; Doz., $84.00
908.
20' × 16 inch
Tabourette.
Price, Each $4.00; Doz., $48.00
920.   44' × 20 inch
Smoker's Cabinet.
Price, Each $10.00; Doz., $120.00

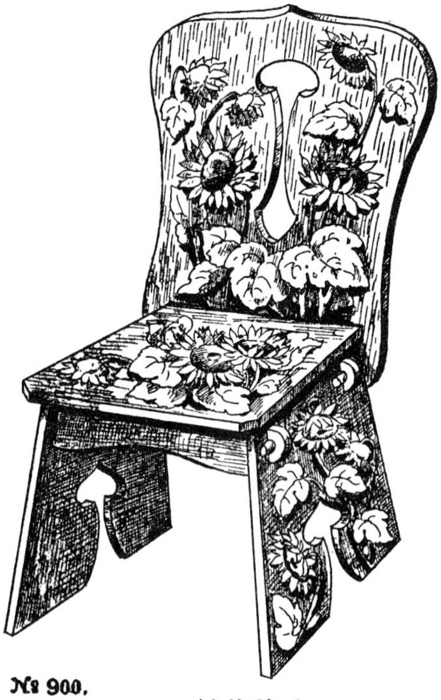

No 900.
37"× 17 inch Hall Chair.
Price, $6.00 Each; Doz., $72.00

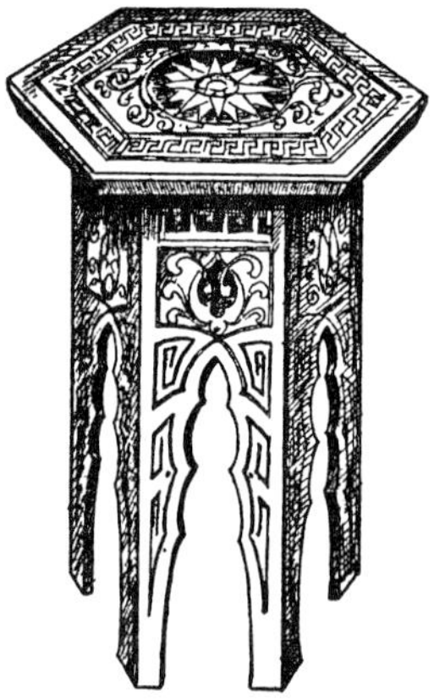

934.
17" × 12 inch
Tabourette.
Price, Each $2.00;
Doz., $24.00

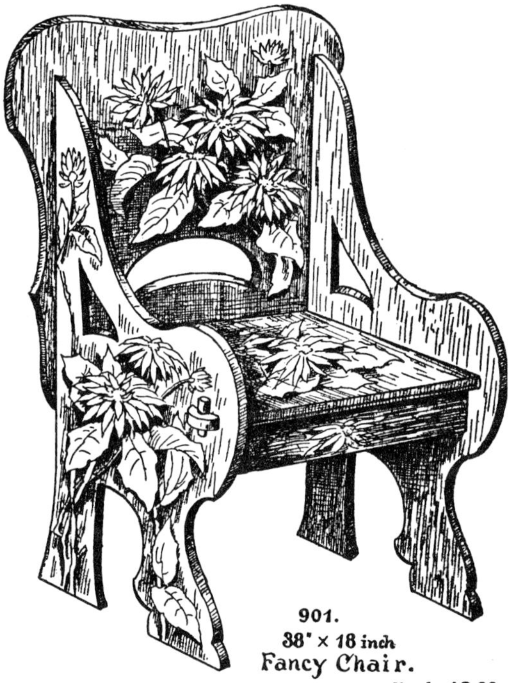

901.
38" × 18 inch
Fancy Chair.
Price, Each $8.00;
Doz., $96.00

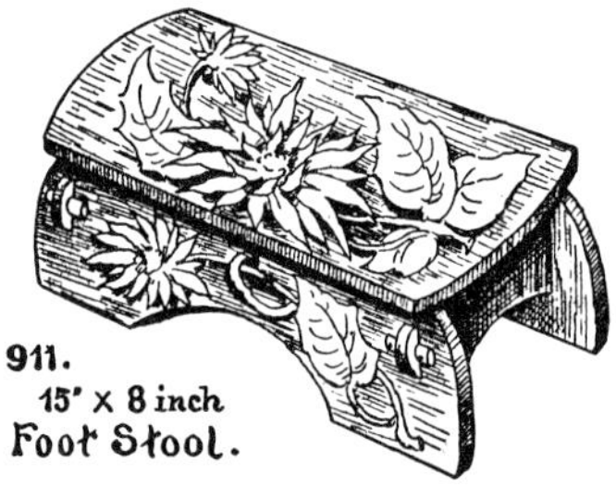

911.
15" × 8 inch
Foot Stool.
Price, Each $1.35;
Doz., $16.00

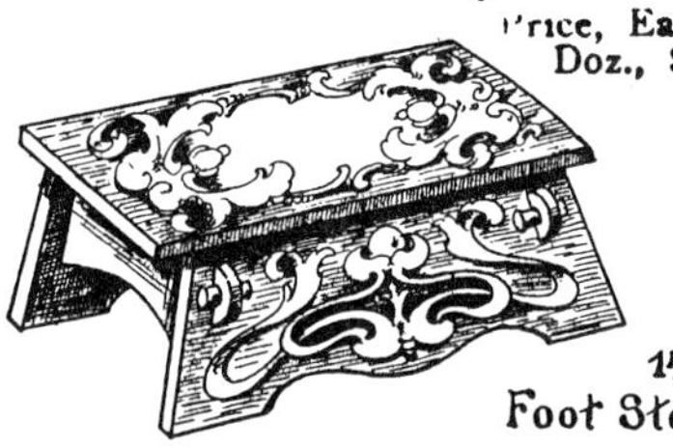

910.
14" × 8 inch
Foot Stool,
Price, Each $1.35;
Doz., $16.00

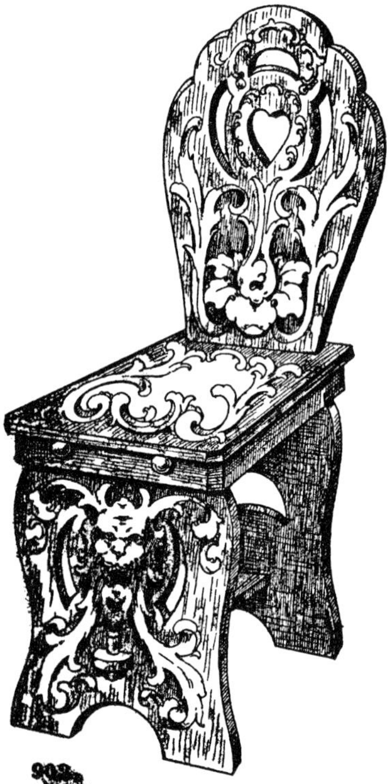

902.
[illegible] inch
Old Dutch Chair.
Price, Each $5.00;
Doz., $60.00

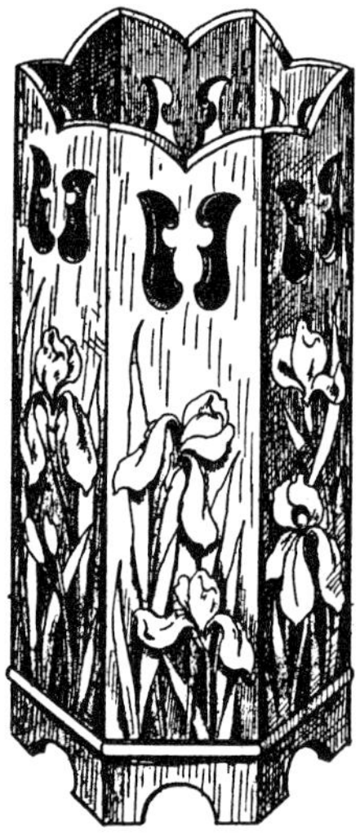

935. 28" × 12 inch
Umbrella Stand.
Price, Each $4.00;
Doz., $48.00

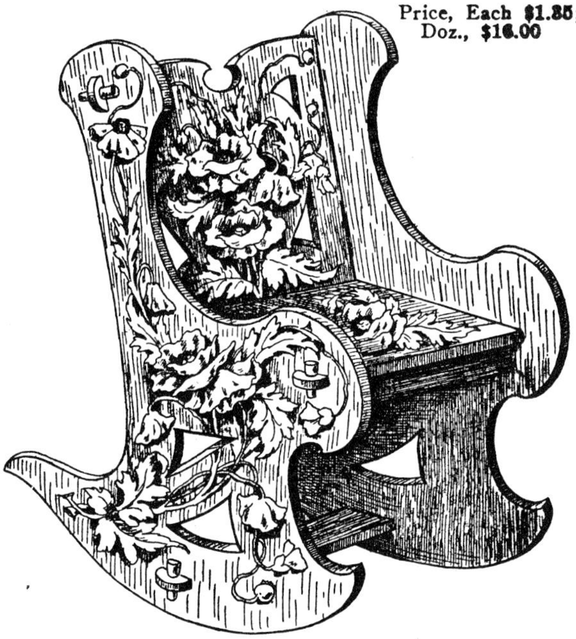

904. 35" × 18 inch
Rocking Chair.
Price, Each $9.00;
Doz., $108.00

OUR FURNITURE PIECES ARE EXTREMELY HANDSOME, WELL DESIGNED AND VERY SUBSTANTIAL. ALL FURNITURE PIECES ARE SHIPPED "KNOCKED DOWN

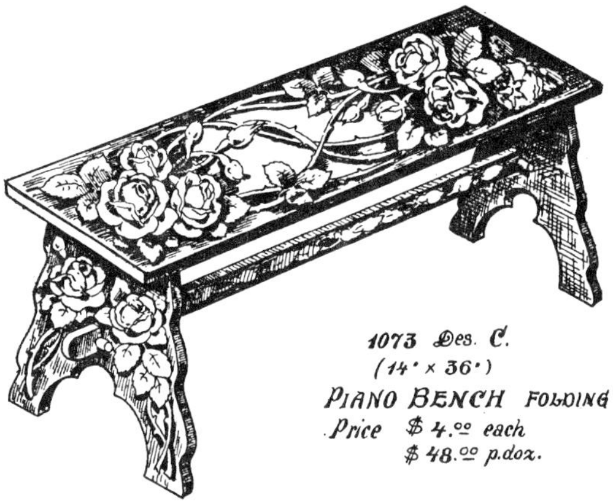

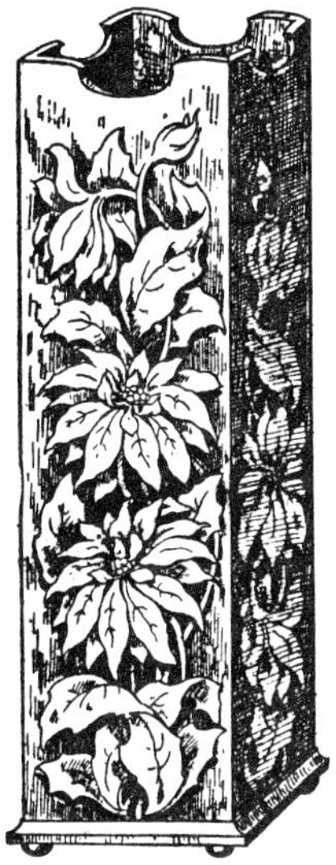

968 Des A.
(9" × 28")
UMBRELLA STAND
Price $ 2.50 each
$ 30.⁰⁰ p.doz

1073 Des. C.
(14" × 36")
PIANO BENCH FOLDING
Price $ 4.⁰⁰ each
$ 48.⁰⁰ p.doz.

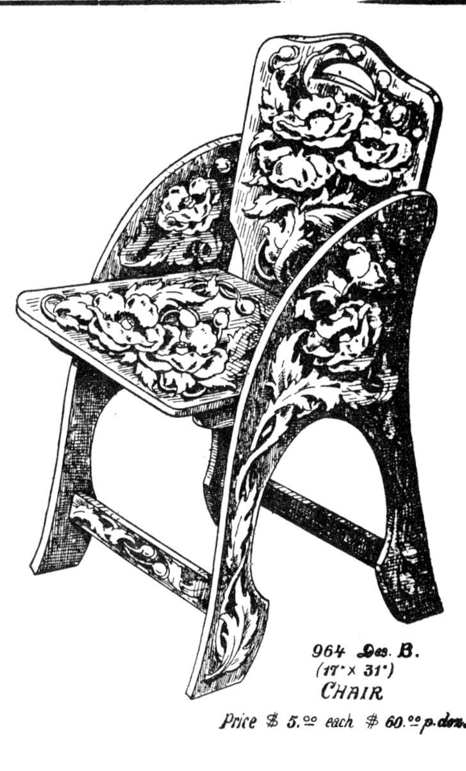

964 Des. B.
(17" × 31")
CHAIR
Price $ 5.⁰⁰ each $ 60.⁰⁰ p.doz.

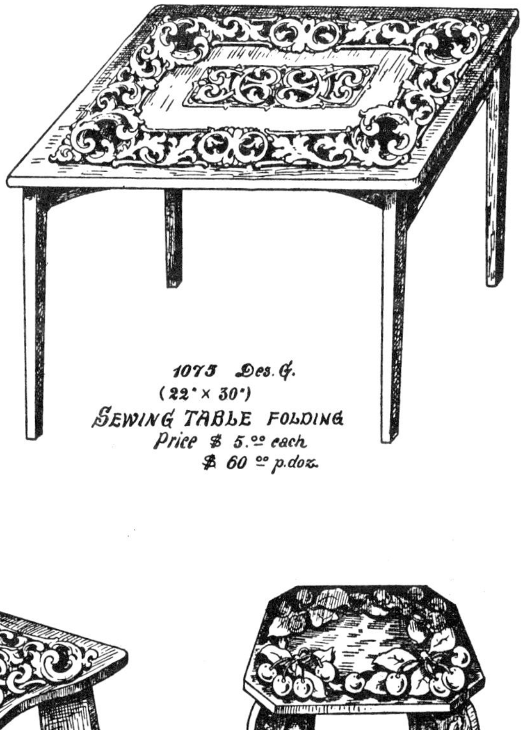

1073 Des. G.
(22" × 30")
SEWING TABLE FOLDING
Price $ 5.⁰⁰ each
$ 60 ⁰⁰ p.doz.

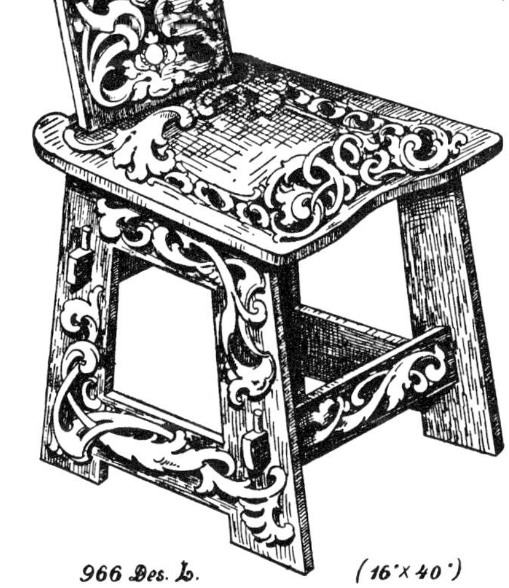

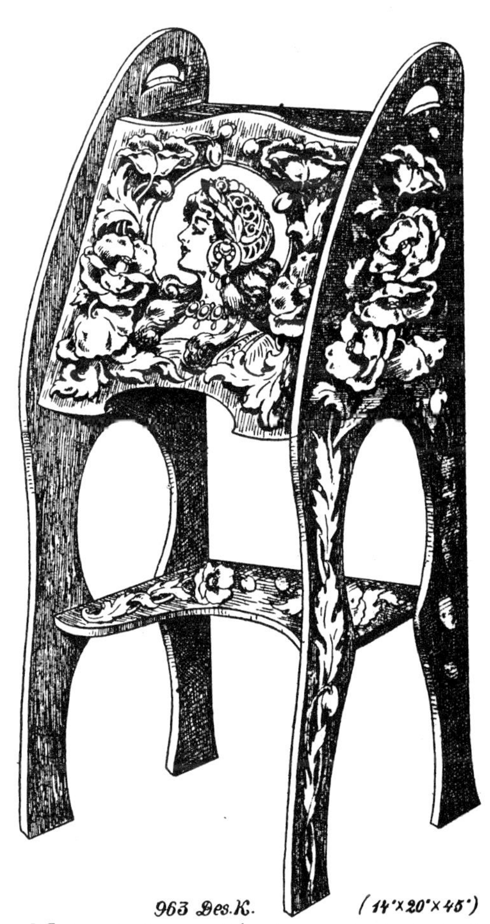

966 Des. L. (16" × 40")
HALL CHAIR Price $ 3.50 each $ 42.⁰⁰ p.doz.

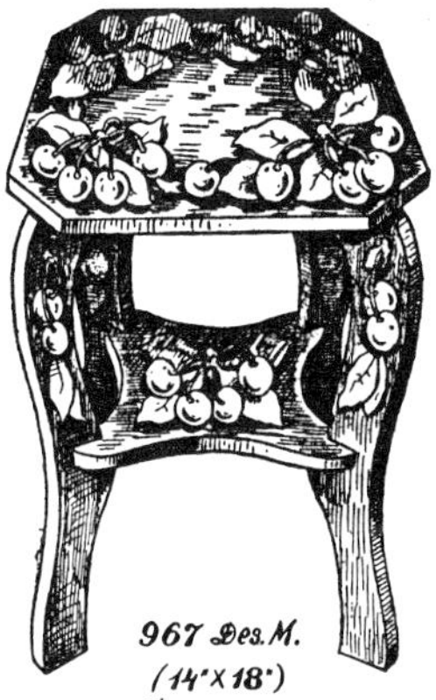

967 Des. M.
(14" × 18")
STOOL
Price $ 2.50 each
$ 30.⁰⁰ p.doz.

963 Des. K. (14" × 20" × 45")
WRITING DESK Price $ 8.⁰⁰ each $ 96.⁰⁰ p.doz.

919
36" × 16 inch
Music Stand (Folding.)
Each $4.00; Doz., $48.00

944   18½" × 18½" (French plate glass 10" × 10")
Three-Ply Basswood Mirror Frames.
Price, Each $2.50; Doz., $30.00

943   18" × 24"   (French plate glass 12" × 18")
Three-Ply Basswood Mirror Frames
Price, Each $5.50; Doz., $66.00

945   20½" × 20½"   (French plate glass 12" × 12")
Three-Ply Basswood Mirror Frames —
with Hat Hooks
Price, Each $5.00; Doz., $60.00

914
47" × 16½" inch
Book Stand
Price, Each $9.00; Doz., $108.00

915.
Music Stand
Price, Each $7.00; Doz., $84.00

916.   36" × 38" × 21 inch
Desk
Price, Each $12.00; Doz., $144.00

923.   28″ x 22 inch
Smoker's Tabourette.
Price, Each $6.00; Doz., $72.00

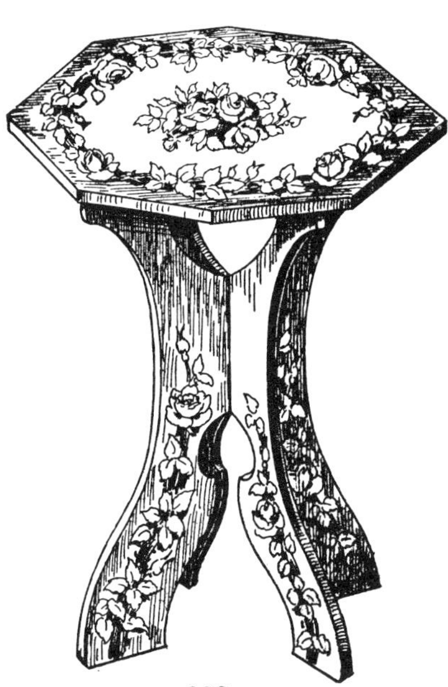

909.
29″ x 22 inch
Table.
Price, Each $4.50;
Doz., $54.00

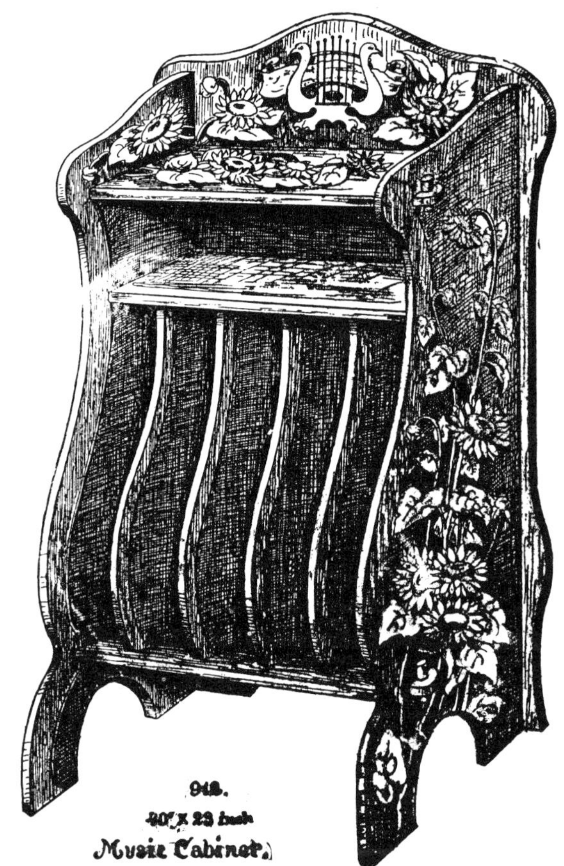

918.
30″ x 23 inch
Music Cabinet.
Price, Each $12.00; Doz., $144.00

903.   39″ x 22 inch
Arm Chair.
Price, Each $9.00; Doz., $108.00

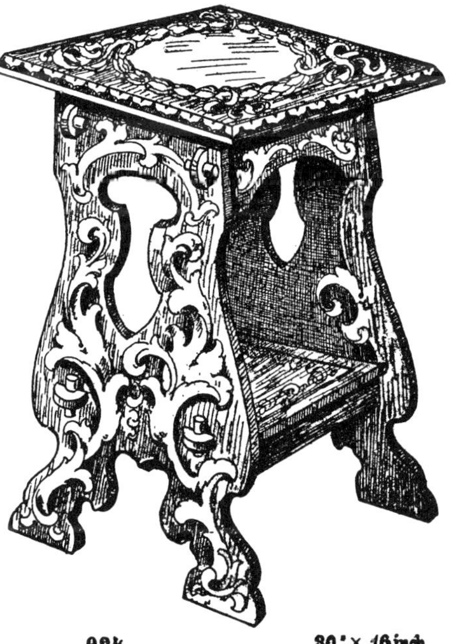

924.   30″ x 16 inch
Table.
Price, Each $6.00; Doz., $72.00

926.   30″ x 12½ inch
Umbrella Stand.
Price, Each $4.50;
Doz., $54.00

925.
16' × 36 inch
Pedestal
Price, Each $8.00; Doz., $96.00

918.
20' × 30' × 30 inch
Combination Playing Table.
Price, Each $16.00; Doz., $192.00

959.
Hat and Coat Rack
Price, **Each $2.00**
Doz., **$24.00**

958.
Hat Rack.
Price, Each $1.00
Doz., $12.00

905.   19' × 25 inch
Corner Seat.
Price, Each $6.00; Doz., $72.00

917.   25' × 43' × 19' inch.
Ladies Desk.
Price, Each $16.00; Doz., $192.00

PYROGRAPHY

CUT PRICE CATALOG NO. 76

BURNING OUTFITS
BASSWOOD ARTICLES FOR DECORATING
LEATHER CUSHION COVERS
COLORS, STAINS, ETC.

This Catalog is a Money Saver for You.

Compare these prices with the former prices you have been paying and you will be satisfied that the big reductions will make and save you money.

IN ORDERING GOODS

Be careful to write your name, town, and state plainly. When money is enclosed, state the amount sent. State how goods are to be shipped---mail, express or freight. In absence of directions we will use our judgment about shipping. Goods by mail require one cent per ounce to cover postage, All claims must be made within five days after receipt of goods. Money should accompany order unless goods are to be sent C. O. D. or arrangements for credit have been made. When goods are to be sent C. O. D., a remittance amounting to one-fourth of the value of the goods must accompany the order. When satisfactory business references are supplied, we are ready to open an account. When credit is extended we require settlements every thirty days.

SAFE DELIVERY GUARANTEED
We guarantee everything we ship you to reach you in perfect condition.

If ever you receive any package from us in a damaged condition, have your freight or express agent make a notation of the damage on receipt he gives you when you pay the charges, send this receipt to us, telling just what is the matter, and we will make it right. In case of express shipments the express agent will give you a receipt on request.

THAYER & CHANDLER

735-739 W. Jackson Boulevard
CHICAGO

PYROGRAPHY OR BURNT WOOD ETCHING, is the art of decorating wood, leather, plush, etc. by burning the design into the article to be decorated.

The origin of this unique scheme of decoration is not as obscure as might at first be supposed; in the days when art and conviviality went hand in hand in the Low Countries, and when in England the tavern was a club-house, it was the wont of artists who gathered over pipe and pot on a winter evening, to exercise their passing inspirations on the walls around them, as mementos of the festive occasion. A poker heated red in the fire-place was their tool. With it they sketched upon the wall the creations of their fancy, and the subject suggested by the discussion—a memory of a scene of nature, an idea of a new style of ornament, and often portraits of each other.

Pyrography is now executed by using Pyro Gas Pencil, Pyro Alco Outfit or Pyrographic Outfits containing a more complete list of materials essential for this fascinating art work. By this method of decorating a great variety of beautiful things can be made for gift purposes or household adornment. Lessons are not necessary. Order an outfit and something to decorate, and with suggestions go to work. All articles are clearly stamped with designs ready for decorating.

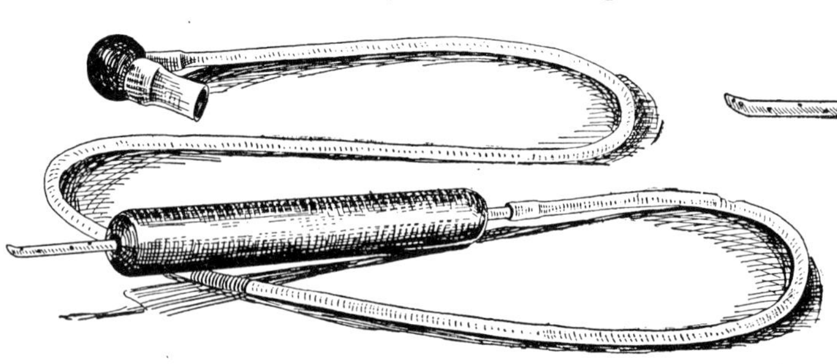

Pyro Gas Pencil.

A very simple and inexpensive instrument for decorating on wood, leather, etc. Socket to be adjusted over gas burner and gas lighted at end of pencil. When sufficiently heated turn gas down low and use Pyro Pencil with same action as that of a pen or pencil. The degree of heat is regulated by the flow of gas.

Complete with 5 feet rubber tubing....................$0.23
Postage, 3c extra.

Illustration half size
Pyro Alco Outfit.

Pyro-Alco Outfit will do the work of more expensive outfits and at a price that anyone can afford to buy. It is simple to operate, has practically indestructible point and does not require the careful attention needed on platinum points. It is complete as shown—has no rubber tubing, bulb or expensive point to wear out. The reservoir is to be filled with wood or grain alcohol. This feeds automatically to the point, through a tube in handle and can be regulated to give any desired heat with a continuous, steady glow. While it does not burn as rapidly as outfits with platinum point, it has about double the speed of Pyro Gas Pencil.

One filling burns about four hours.

Made of burnished brass fitted with polished wood handle. Outfit consists of **burning machine, alcohol lamp, small wrench, small funnel, Pelican instruction book** and directions. All contained in neat cardboard box.
Price, per outfit complete.........................$0.79
Postage 10c extra.
Extra Points .... .18

Assortments of Basswood Articles for Decorating

Fifteen Piece Assortment, $2.35.

FEA624. Assortment, stamped, **$2.35.** If bought by the piece would cost **$2.75.** Includes 1 stool, 14½ inches; 1 book rack, 15 inches; 1 glove box, 10 inches; handkerchief box, 6 inches; 1 oval panel, 10x13½ inches; 1 oval panel, 4x7 inches; 1 panel, 4x6 inches; 3 circles, 4 inches; 1 square cabinet frame, 8x10 inches; 1 oval cabinet frame, 8x10 inches, and two post cards.

If items shown in these assortments are out of stock we will substitute a similar article as good or better in value.

Ten Piece Assortment, $2.10.

FDA618. Assortment, stamped, **$2.10.** If bought by the piece would cost **$2.45.** Includes 1 stool, 14½ inches; 1 book rack, 15 inches; 1 handkerchief box, 6 inches; 1 glove box, 10 inches; 1 match hanger, 7x12 inches; 1 frame, 8 inches; 1 panel, 4x6 inches; 1 ladies collar box, 6 inches; 1 circle, 10 inches, and 1 tie rack, 15 inches.

White Basswood Boxes for Pyrographic Decoration

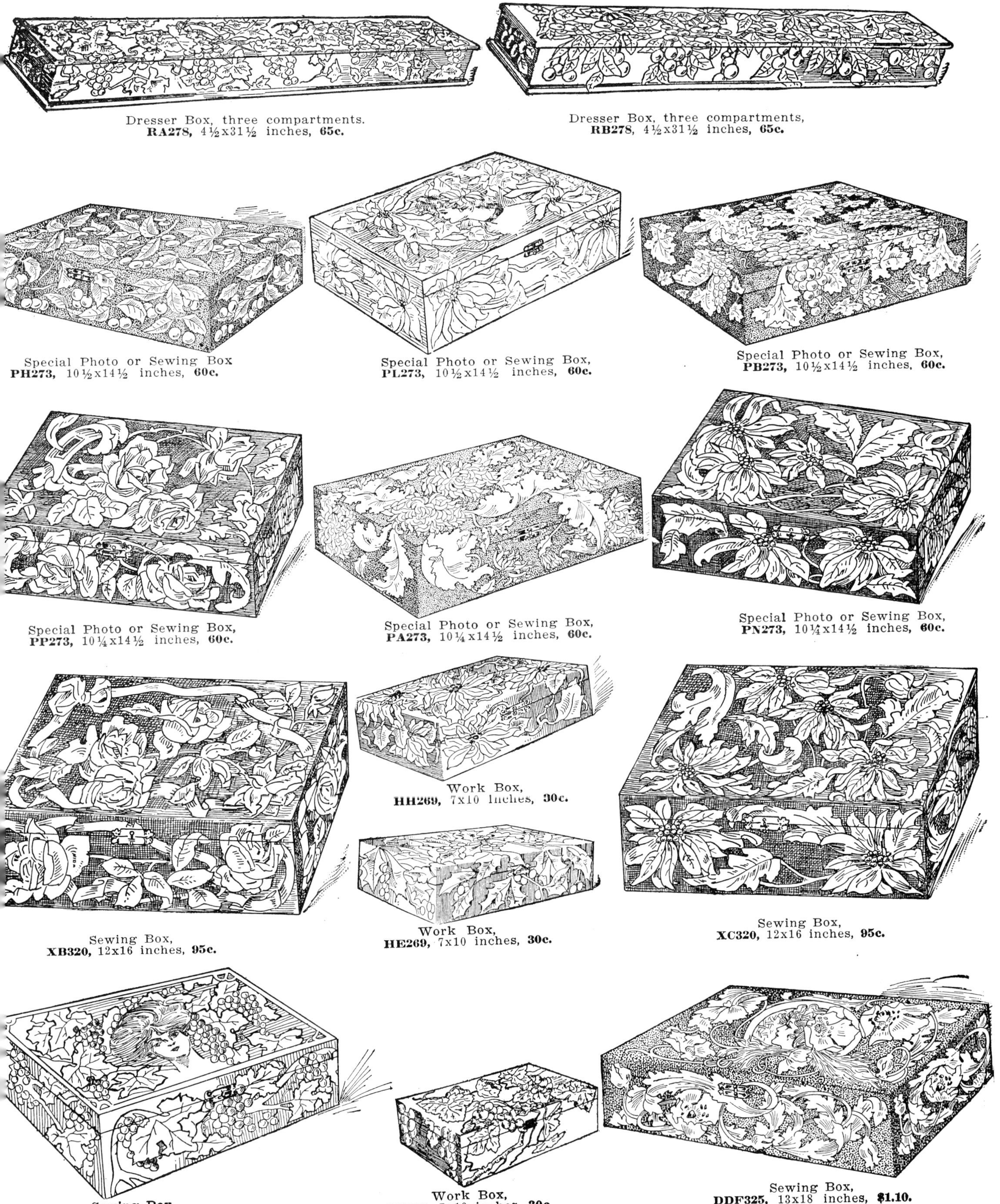

Dresser Box, three compartments.
RA278, 4½x31½ inches, **65c.**

Dresser Box, three compartments,
RB278, 4½x31½ inches, **65c.**

Special Photo or Sewing Box
PH273, 10½x14½ inches, **60c.**

Special Photo or Sewing Box,
PL273, 10½x14½ inches, **60c.**

Special Photo or Sewing Box,
PB273, 10½x14½ inches, **60c.**

Special Photo or Sewing Box,
PP273, 10¼x14½ inches, **60c.**

Special Photo or Sewing Box,
PA273, 10¼x14½ inches, **60c.**

Special Photo or Sewing Box,
PN273, 10¼x14½ inches, **60c.**

Sewing Box,
XB320, 12x16 inches, **95c.**

Work Box,
HH269, 7x10 inches, **30c.**

Work Box,
HE269, 7x10 inches, **30c.**

Sewing Box,
XC320, 12x16 inches, **95c.**

Sewing Box,
DDB325, 13x18 inches, **$1.10.**

Work Box,
HB269, 7x10 inches, **30c.**

Sewing Box,
DDF325, 13x18 inches, **$1.10.**

Basswood Articles for Pyrographic Decoration

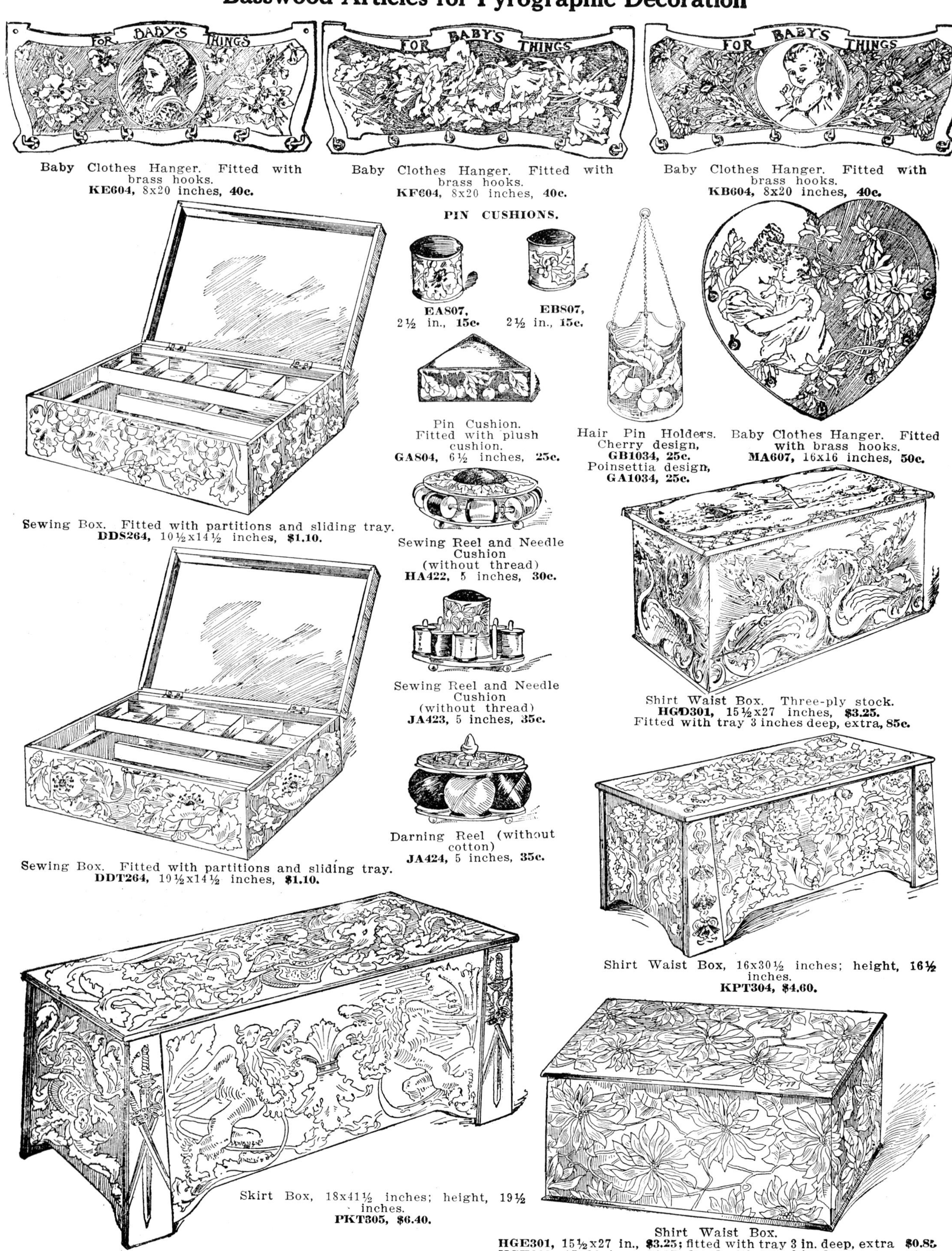

Baby Clothes Hanger. Fitted with brass hooks.
KE604, 8x20 inches, **40c.**

Baby Clothes Hanger. Fitted with brass hooks.
KF604, 8x20 inches, **40c.**

Baby Clothes Hanger. Fitted with brass hooks.
KB604, 8x20 inches, **40c.**

Sewing Box. Fitted with partitions and sliding tray.
DDS264, 10½x14½ inches, **$1.10.**

Sewing Box. Fitted with partitions and sliding tray.
DDT264, 10½x14½ inches, **$1.10.**

PIN CUSHIONS.

EA807, 2½ in., **15c.**

EB807, 2½ in., **15c.**

Pin Cushion. Fitted with plush cushion.
GA804, 6½ inches, **25c.**

Sewing Reel and Needle Cushion (without thread)
HA422, 5 inches, **30c.**

Sewing Reel and Needle Cushion (without thread)
JA423, 5 inches, **35c.**

Darning Reel (without cotton)
JA424, 5 inches, **35c.**

Hair Pin Holders. Cherry design, **GB1034**, 25c.
Poinsettia design, **GA1034**, 25c.

Baby Clothes Hanger. Fitted with brass hooks.
MA607, 16x16 inches, **50c.**

Shirt Waist Box. Three-ply stock.
HGD301, 15½x27 inches, **$3.25.**
Fitted with tray 3 inches deep, extra, 85c.

Shirt Waist Box, 16x30½ inches; height, 16½ inches.
KPT304, **$4.60.**

Skirt Box, 18x41½ inches; height, 19½ inches.
PKT305, **$6.40.**

Shirt Waist Box.
HGE301, 15½x27 in., **$3.25**; fitted with tray 3 in. deep, extra **$0.85**
KGE302, 17x36 in., **$4.25**; fitted with tray 3 in. deep, extra **1.15**
MWE303, 18x45 in., **$5.90**; fitted with tray 3 in. deep, extra **1.40**

Basswood Articles for Pyrographic Decoration
White Holly Hat Pins
Gold Plated Mounts.

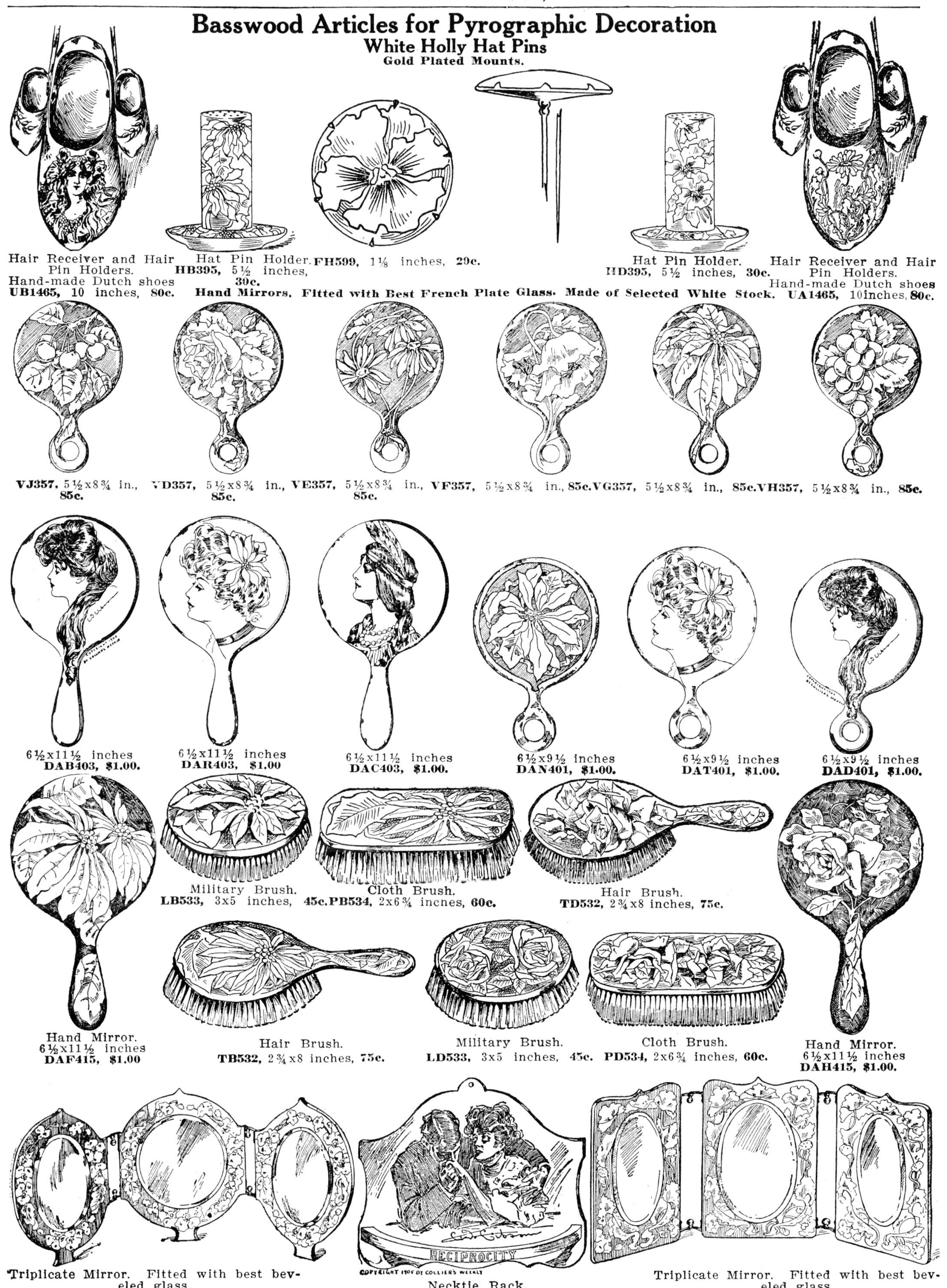

Hair Receiver and Hair Pin Holders. Hand-made Dutch shoes **UB1465,** 10 inches, **80c.**

Hat Pin Holder. **HB395,** 5½ inches, **30c.**

FH599, 1⅛ inches, **29c.**

Hat Pin Holder. **HD395,** 5½ inches, **30c.**

Hair Receiver and Hair Pin Holders. Hand-made Dutch shoes **UA1465,** 10 inches, **80c.**

Hand Mirrors. Fitted with Best French Plate Glass. Made of Selected White Stock.

VJ357, 5½ x 8¾ in., **85c.**   **VD357,** 5½ x 8¾ in., **85c.**   **VE357,** 5½ x 8¾ in., **85c.**   **VF357,** 5½ x 8¾ in., **85c.**   **VG357,** 5½ x 8¾ in., **85c.**   **VH357,** 5½ x 8¾ in., **85c.**

6½ x 11½ inches **DAB403, $1.00.**   6½ x 11½ inches **DAR403, $1.00**   6½ x 11½ inches **DAC403, $1.00.**   6½ x 9½ inches **DAN401, $1.00.**   6½ x 9½ inches **DAT401, $1.00.**   6½ x 9½ inches **DAD401, $1.00.**

Military Brush. **LB533,** 3x5 inches, **45c.**   Cloth Brush. **PB534,** 2x6¾ inches, **60c.**   Hair Brush. **TD532,** 2¾x8 inches, **75c.**

Hand Mirror. 6½ x 11½ inches **DAF415, $1.00**

Hair Brush. **TB532,** 2¾x8 inches, **75c.**   Military Brush. **LD533,** 3x5 inches, **45c.**   Cloth Brush. **PD534,** 2x6¾ inches, **60c.**

Hand Mirror. 6½ x 11½ inches **DAH415, $1.00.**

Triplicate Mirror. Fitted with best beveled glass. **FKA524,** 9x26¼ inches, **$2.40.**

Necktie Rack. **JA473,** 9x11 inches, **35c.**

Triplicate Mirror. Fitted with best beveled glass. **FKA525,** 9½x23 inches, **$2.40.**

Basswood Articles, for Pyrographic Decoration
HAIR RIBBON HOLDERS

A new and popular article in which girls will take a keen interest. While novel in every sense of the word, it is an article of positive utility. Made of clear white basswood and appropriately designed. Shapes 1497-1498 have brass extension hooks; 1517 has wood extension knobs and rod.

EA1497, 12 inches, 15c.

MA1517, 6x23 inches, 50c.

EB1498, 12 inches, 15c.

NECKTIE RACKS

These popular novelties are new in both shape and design. They are made of white basswood clearly stamped with artistic designs and are offered at prices which represent splendid values. Shapes 461-611-1492-1494-1495-1496 have wood extension knobs and rod, other shapes have metal extension rod.

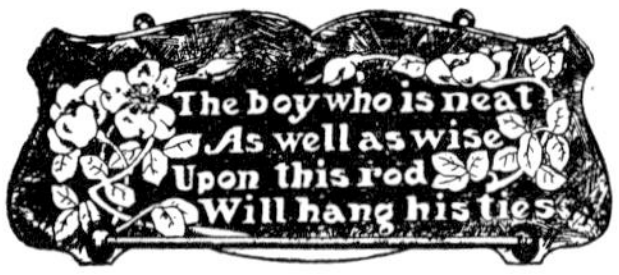

EB1496, 12 inches, 15c.

EA1495, 12 inches, 15c.

EB1494, 15 inches, 15c.

EA1494, 15 inches, 15c.

MG475, 9x23¼ inches, 50c.

HA1518, 14 inches, 30c.

KB1481, 7x19 inches, 40c.

KA1481, 7x19 inches, 40c.

JA611, 7½x13 inches, 35c.

MA1492, Towel Rack, 20½ inches, 50c.

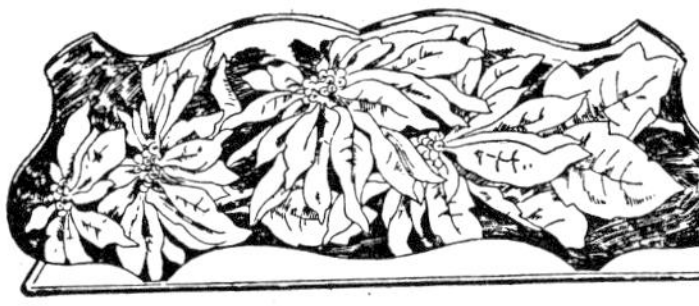

HC1480, 5½x15½ inches, 30c.

NA1487, 12x23 inches, 55c.

HB1480, 5½x15½ inches, 30c.

NA476, 11x23¼ inches, 55c.

Towel Rack. Fitted with nickel plated rod.
WD566, 14x22 inches, 90c.

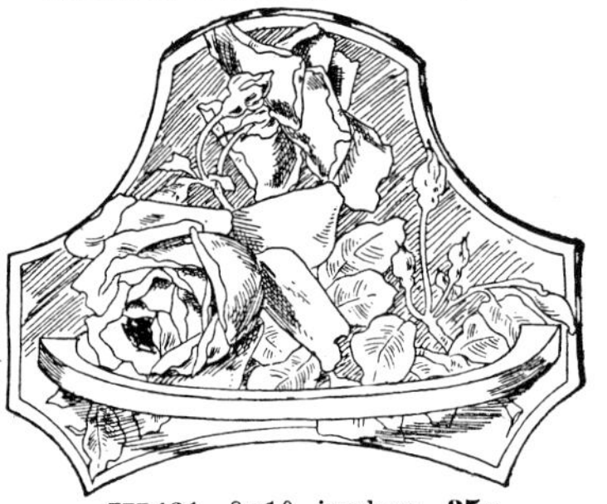

JK461, 8x10 inches, 35c.

Towel Rack. Fitted with nickel plated rod.
WB566, 14x22 inches, 80c.

Basswood Articles for Pyrographic Decoration

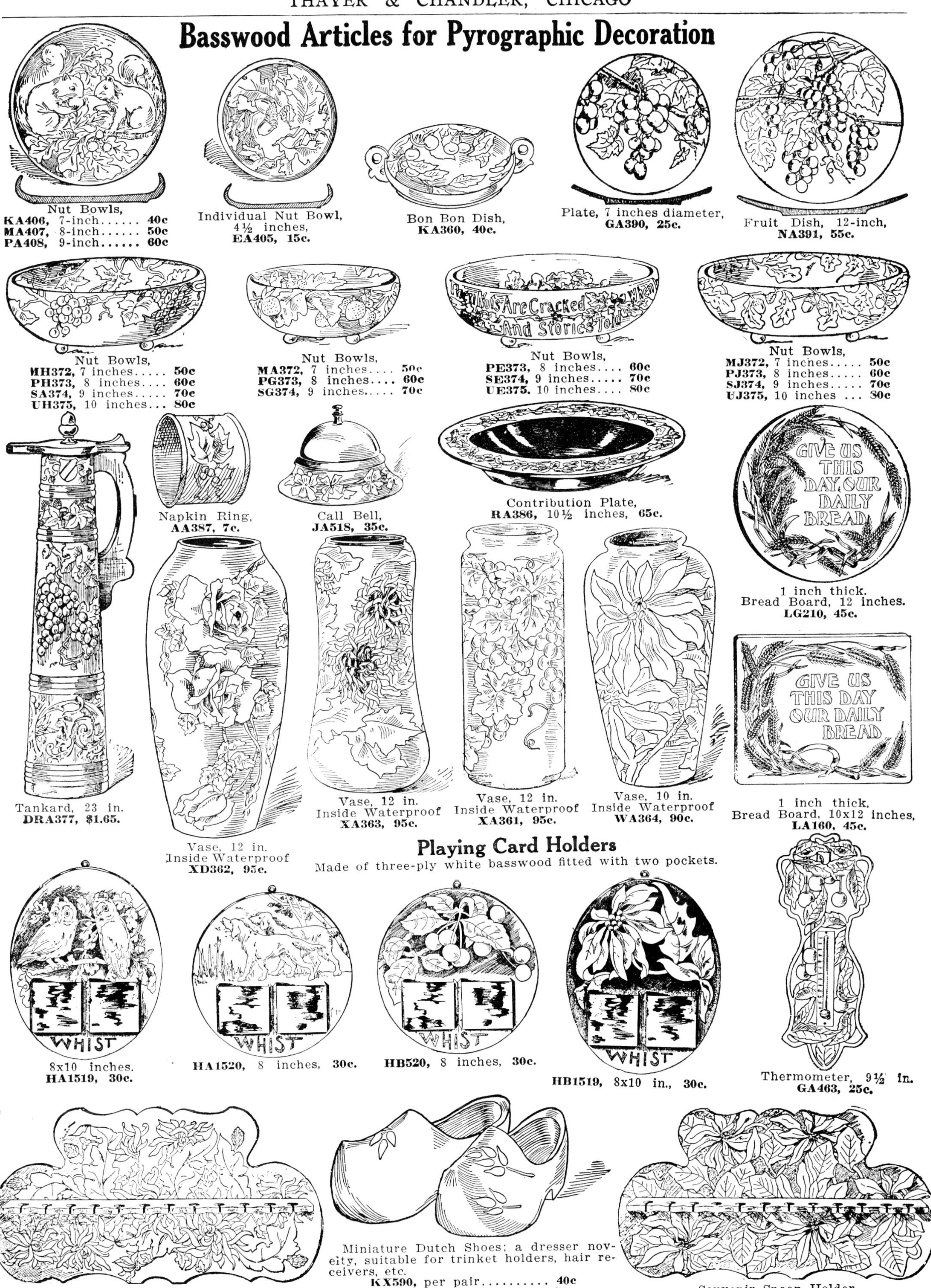

Nut Bowls,
KA406, 7-inch...... **40c**
MA407, 8-inch...... **50c**
PA408, 9-inch...... **60c**

Individual Nut Bowl,
4½ inches,
EA405, 15c.

Bon Bon Dish,
KA360, 40c.

Plate, 7 inches diameter,
GA390, 25c.

Fruit Dish, 12-inch,
NA391, 55c.

Nut Bowls,
ИН372, 7 inches..... **50c**
PH373, 8 inches.... **60c**
SA374, 9 inches..... **70c**
UH375, 10 inches... **80c**

Nut Bowls,
MA372, 7 inches.... **50c**
PG373, 8 inches.... **60c**
SG374, 9 inches..... **70c**

Nut Bowls,
PE373, 8 inches.... **60c**
SE374, 9 inches..... **70c**
UE375, 10 inches... **80c**

Nut Bowls,
MJ372, 7 inches..... **50c**
PJ373, 8 inches..... **60c**
SJ374, 9 inches..... **70c**
UJ375, 10 inches ... **80c**

Napkin Ring,
AA387, 7c.

Call Bell,
JA518, 35c.

Contribution Plate,
RA386, 10½ inches, 65c.

1 inch thick.
Bread Board, 12 inches.
LG210, 45c.

Tankard, 23 in.
DRA377, $1.65.

Vase, 12 in.
Inside Waterproof
XA363, 95c.

Vase, 12 in.
Inside Waterproof
XA361, 95c.

Vase, 10 in.
Inside Waterproof
WA364, 90c.

1 inch thick.
Bread Board, 10x12 inches,
LA160, 45c.

Vase, 12 in.
Inside Waterproof
XD362, 95c.

Playing Card Holders

Made of three-ply white basswood fitted with two pockets.

8x10 inches.
HA1519, 30c.

HA1520, 8 inches, **30c.**

HB520, 8 inches, **30c.**

HB1519, 8x10 in., **30c.**

Thermometer, 9½ in.
GA463, 25c.

Souvenir Spoon Holder.
PA479, 13x24½ inches, 60c.

Miniature Dutch Shoes; a dresser nov-
elty, suitable for trinket holders, hair re-
ceivers, etc.
KX590, per pair........ **40c**
MX591, per pair........ **50c**
PX592, per pair........ **60c**

Souvenir Spoon Holder.
PB479, 13x24½ inches, 60c.

Basswood Trays for Pyrographic
Decoration

Pen Tray.
EB448, 3⅛x9¼ inches, **15c.**

Pen Tray, brass edges.
JB1429, 4½x10½ inches, **35c.**

Comb and Brush Tra
KE442, 9x13 inches, **40**

Comb and Brush Tray.
KD442, 9x13 inches, **40c.**

Pen Tray, brass edge.
JA1429, 4½x10½ inches, **35c.**

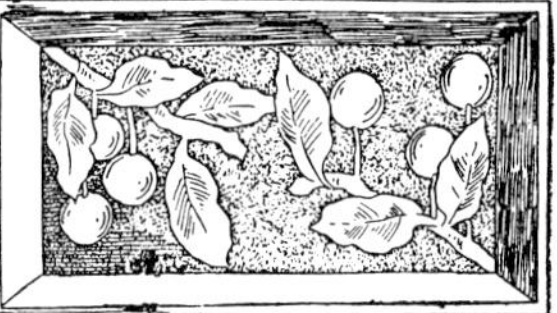

Cigar Tray.
ED441, 4¼x7½ inches, **15c.**

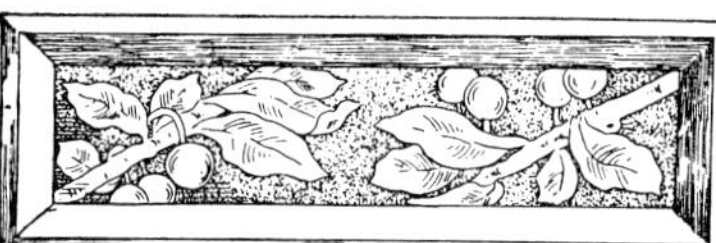

Pen Tray.
ED440, 3¼x9½ inches, **15c.**

Hair Pin Tray.
GA1427, 3½x7½ inches.

Card Tray.
EB449, 4x7 inches, **15c.**

Tea Tray. Burnished brass edge and handles.
FGD447, 16x24 inches, **$2.25.**
Fitted with glass top, 75c extra.

Comb and Brush Tra
JB1425, 9x12 inches, **3**

Tea Tray. Burnished brass edge.
DJA1433, 10½x14½ inches, **$1.35.**

Brush and Comb Tray.
Burnished brass edge.
UB1431, 7½x15 inches, **80c.**

Tea Tray. Burnished brass edge.
DJB1413, 10½x14½ inches, **$1.35.**

Comb and Brush Tray.
JA1425, 9x12 inches, **35c.**

Brush and Comb Tray.
Burnished brass edge.
UA1431, 7½x15 inches, **80c.**

Tea Tray.
DMA1426, 16x22 inches, **$1.50.**

Serving Tray.
Burnished brass edge and handles.
FDA445, 18 inches, **$2.10.**
Fitted with glass top, 65c extra.

Serving Tray.
Burnished brass edge and handle.
DRA443, 14 inches, **$1.65.**
Fitted with glass top, 30c extra.

Tea Tray.
Burnished brass edge and handles.
FGB447, 16x24 inches, **$2.25.**
Fitted with glass top, 75c extra.

Basswood Articles for Pyrographic Decoration

Smoker's Set, 5 pieces.
DGA384, $1.25.

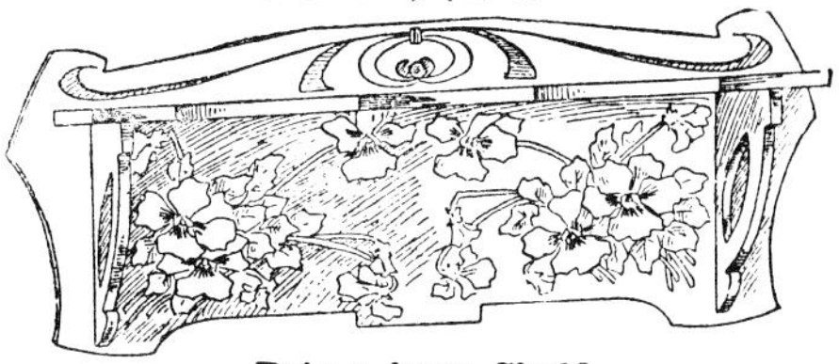

Whisk Broom Holder.
Genuine hand-made
Dutch shoes. Whitewood.
JA550, 10 inches, 35c.

Scrap Basket.
RB523, 9x9½ inches, 65c.

Whisk Broom Holder.
JB507, 8x10 inches, 35c.

Bric-a-brac Shelf.
UA759, 8x20 inches, 80c.

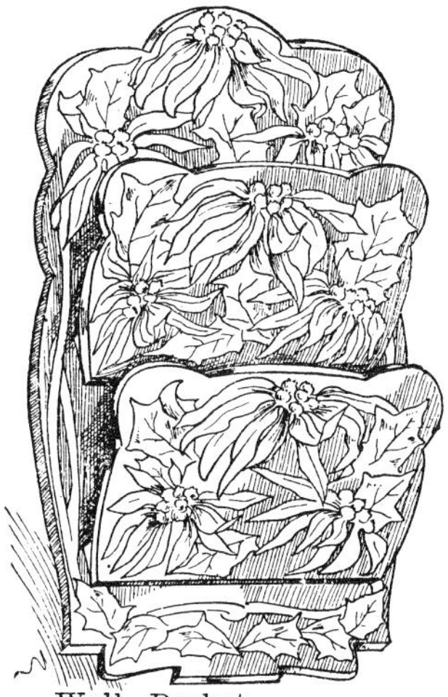

Wall Pocket.
14x24 inches
DJB760, $1.35.

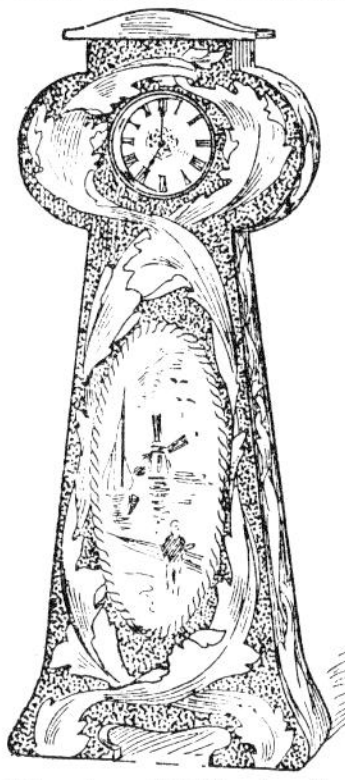

Clock, 18½ inches.
DVU717, $1.85.

Clock, 15 inches.
DTT716, $1.75.

Clock, 18½ inches.
DVV717, $1.85.

Clock, 14 inches.
DXA1522, $1.95.

Wall Pocket.
14x24 inches
DJA760, $1.35.

SCRAP BASKETS

The remarkable values in these baskets is the result of a strong effort to produce this item in the newest, up-to-date style at a popular price. Made of selected kiln-dried white basswood beautifully designed in popular floral and fruit effects. A very artistic and inexpensive piece for any room.　　　Shipped knocked down.

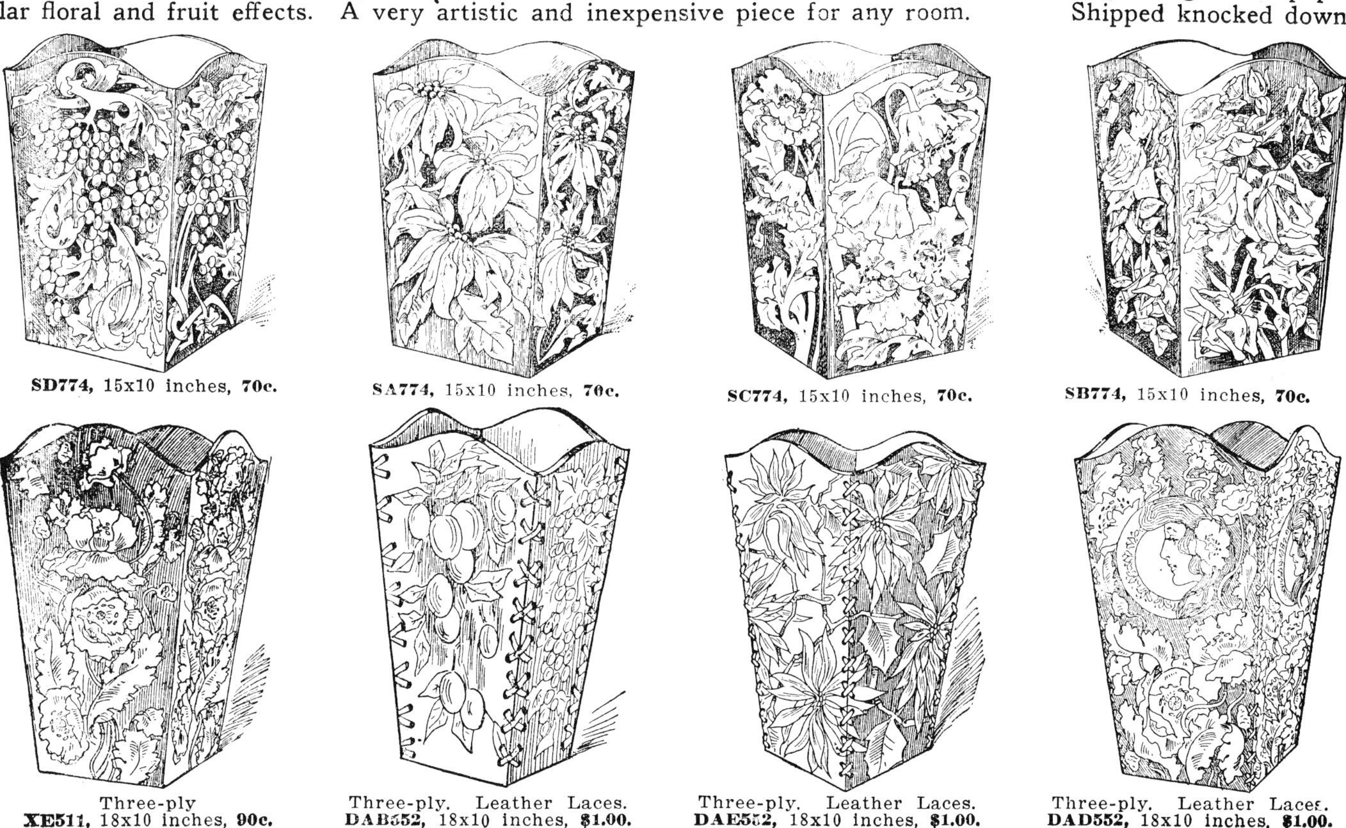

SD774, 15x10 inches, 70c.

SA774, 15x10 inches, 70c.

SC774, 15x10 inches, 70c.

SB774, 15x10 inches, 70c.

Three-ply
XE511, 18x10 inches, 90c.

Three-ply. Leather Laces.
DAB552, 18x10 inches, $1.00.

Three-ply. Leather Laces.
DAE552, 18x10 inches, $1.00.

Three-ply. Leather Laces.
DAD552, 18x10 inches, $1.00.

Basswood Articles for Pyrographic Decoration

Coat and Hat Rack. Fitted with elaborate combination hook.
WD483, 14 inches, 90c.

Coat and Hat Rack. Oxidized hooks.
DPB613, 10x30 inches, $1.60.

Coat and Hat Rack. Fitted with elaborate combination hook.
WB483, 14 inches, 90c.

Mirror and Frame. Outside, 18½x18½ inches; mirror, 11½x11½ inches.
FJA84, $2.35.

Coat and Hat Rack. Fitted with elaborate combination hook.
WE483, 14 inches, 90c.

Coat and Hat Rack. Fitted with Oxidized hooks.
FAB763, 20x30 inches, $2.00.

Hall Mirror. Outside, 20x22; mirror, 11½x11½. Fitted with brass combination hat and coat hooks.
FVF83 . . . .**$2.85**

Mirror and Frame. Outside, 20½x20½ inches; mirror, 11½x11½ inches. Fitted with brass combination hat hooks.
FVA85 . . . .**$2.85**

Mirror and Frame. Outside, 18x24 inches; mirror, 12x18 inches.
HRA32

Hall Mirror. Outside, 20x22; mirror, 11½x11½. Fitted with brass combination hat and coat hooks.
FVG83 . . . .**$2.85**

Hall Mirror and Frame. Outside, 20x30 inches; glass, 14x24 inches.
MMB81 . . . .**$5.50**

Checker Board.
PB214, 20x20 inches, 60c.

Basswood Articles for Pyrographic Decoration

Foot Stool, shipped K. D.
RT625, 10x13 inches, 65c.

Foot Stool. Shipped K. D.
10x13 inches,
RA625, 65c.

Coat and Hat Rack.
DUA564, 15x33 inches, $1.80.

Stool or Jardiniere
Stand, shipped K. D.
12x14½ inches,
VU629, 85c.

Stool or Jardiniere
Stand, shipped K. D.
12x14½ inches,
VU630, 85c.

Stool or Jardiniere
Stand, shipped K. D.
14x14½ inches,
VA627, 85c.

Umbrella Stand, 24
inches. Fitted with
metal pan.
DVT689, $1.85.

Tabourette, 14x17 inches
DRA631, $1.65.

Umbrella Stand, 22
inches. Fitted with
metal pan.
DVT688, $1.85.

Tabourette, 14x17 inches
DRB631, $1.85.

Tabourette
DRA773, 17x14 inches, $1.65

Tabourette
DRB773, 17x14 inches, $1.65

Tabourette
DLB754, 15x17 inches, $1.45

Tabourette
DRC773, 17x14 inches, $1.65

Tabourette
DLD754, 15x17 inches, $1.45

Tabourette
DWV633, 16x19 inches, $1.90

Tabourette
DWT632, 16x19 inches, $1.90

Tabourette
DLA754, 15x17 inches, $1.45

Basswood Articles for Pyrographic Decoration

Stool, 13x14½, shipped K. D.
VB628, stamped, **85c.**

Palm Stand.
DWT747, 19 inches, **$1.90.**

Fern Stand.
DWU747, 19 inches, **$1.90.**

Stool or Jardiniere Stand
shipped K. D.
VT629, 12x14½ inches, **85c.**

Pedestal, 38 inches; top, 12x
12 inches.
FWP68., **$2.90.**

Screen.
FGT723, 24x35½ inches, **$2.25.**

Tea Table.   **HTT648**, 20x30 inches, **$3.75.**

Screen.
FXT700, 23x48¼ inches, **$2.95.**

Pedestal, 38 inches; top, 12x
12 inches.
FWB682, **$2.90.**

Pedestal, height 37 inches;
top, 12 inches.
FWT728, **$2.90.**

Writing Desk and Book
Shelves. Fitted with Lock and
Key. Drop front, 29x50 inches;
12 inches deep.
MGA775, **$5.25.**

Basswood Articles for Pyrographic Decoration

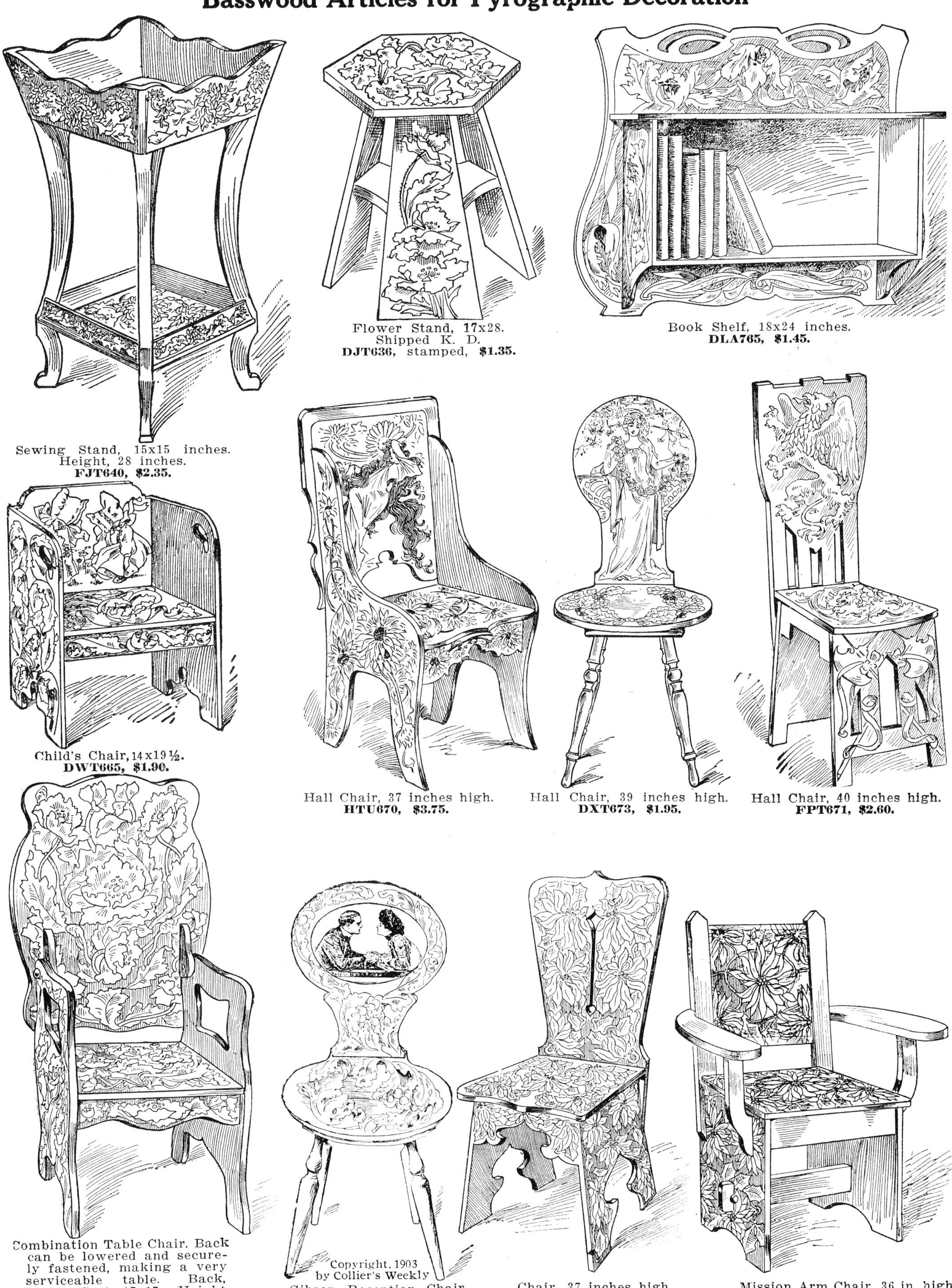

Sewing Stand, 15x15 inches.
Height, 28 inches.
FJT640, $2.35.

Flower Stand, 17x28.
Shipped K. D.
DJT636, stamped, $1.35.

Book Shelf, 18x24 inches.
DLA765, $1.45.

Child's Chair, 14x19½.
DWT665, $1.90.

Hall Chair, 37 inches high.
HTU670, $3.75.

Hall Chair, 39 inches high.
DXT673, $1.95.

Hall Chair, 40 inches high.
FPT671, $2.60.

Combination Table Chair. Back can be lowered and securely fastened, making a very serviceable table. Back, 24x30. Seat, 17x17. Height as table, 30 inches.
KXT676, $4.95.

Copyright, 1903
by Collier's Weekly
Gibson Reception Chair, 37½ inches high.
DXT737, $1.95.

Chair, 37 inches high.
FTU672, $2.75.

Mission Arm Chair, 36 in. high
HVU667, $3.85.

Basswood Articles for Pyrographic Decoration

Tea or Smoker's Table, 25x27.
Fitted with lock and key.
HXB660, $3.95.

Sewing Table, 16x30 inches,
height 30 inches. Fitted
with two sliding trays. End
pockets. **MGU642, $5.25.**

Tea or Smoker's Table, 25x2
Fitted with lock and key.
HXA660, $3.95.

Tea Table, 26x31 inches.
FWT647, $2.90.

Center Table, 22 in. diameter, 28 in. high.
DXT645, $1.95.

Center Table. Height, 29 in; top, 23½ in
FMA767, $2.50.

Center Table, 24 in. diameter, 28 in. high.
DXT646, $1.95.

Tea Table.
Height, 29 inches; top, 20x30 inches.
HTA769, $3.75.

Priscilla Sewing Table.
Top, 16x28; height, 28 inch
Fitted with two sliding tray
KWT641, $4.90.

Basswood Articles for Pyrographic Decoration

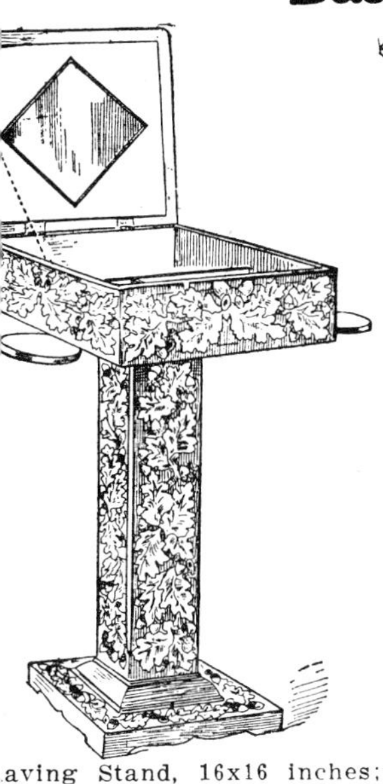

Shaving Stand, 16x16 inches; height, open, 45 inches; fitted with mirror and two swinging shelves. **KST681, $4.70.**

Piano Bench, 14x36 inches, box seat, 1⅛-inch stock. **KGT662, $4.25.**

Piano Bench, 14x36 inches. 1⅛-inch stock. **FTT661, $2.75.**

Music Cabinet, 42 inches high. Fitted with 6 shelves, lock and key. **SJT699, $7.35.**

Music Cabinet, 18x36 inches. Fitted with lock and key. **MTT744, $5.75.**

Scrap Basket, 12 in. Shipped K. D. **SA510, 70c.**

Music Stand, 16x36 inches. **FMU690, $2.50.**

Hall Clock, 19x90 inches. Fitted with eight-day movement, hour and half-hour strike, cathedral gong. **YT698, $16.50.**

Magazine Stand, 13½x43. **HJD683, $3.35.**

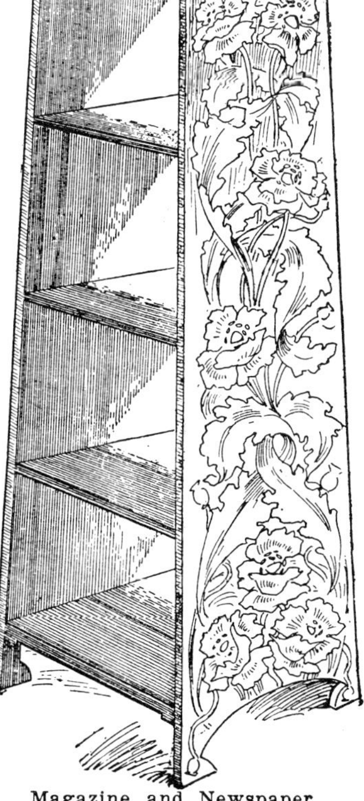

Magazine and Newspaper Stand, 13½x43 inches. **HJU683, $3.35.**

Music Stand, 16x36 inches. **FMT690, $2.50.**

Three-Ply White Basswood Panels for Pyrographic Decoration

Reciprocity
GA1208, 10 inches, **25c**

Psyche at nature's mirror
GB1208, 10 inches, **25c**

Madonna and Child
GC1208, 10 inches, **25c**

American Girl
GD1208, 10 inches, **25c**

Magdalen
KC1201, 15 inches, **40c**

St. Cecelia
KE1201, 15 inches, **40c**

Faith
KF1201, 15 inches, **40c**

Spring Breezes
KD1201, 15 inches, **40c**

Christ in Gethsemane
GN169, 12x14 inches, **25c**
AF181, 16x20 inches, **48c**

Dutch Fishing Boat
KB1201, 15 inches, **40c**

EV130, 8 inches, **15c**
AN139, 16 inches, **43c**

EA130, 8 inches, **15c**
GA135, 12 inches, **25c**
AA139, 16 inches, **43c**

EW130, 8 inches, **15c**
AP139, 16 inches, **43c**

Three-Ply Basswood Panels for Pyrographic Decoration

These Gibson copyrights fully protected.   We have the exclusive right to reproduce these subjects for pyrographic work.

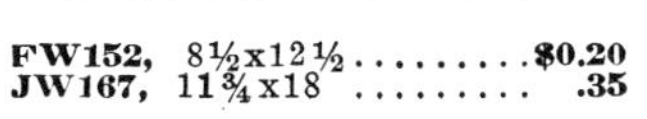

FW152, 8½x12½ **$0.20**
JW167, 11¾x18 .... .35

FE155, 8½x12½ inches... **$0.20**
JE167, 11¾x18 inches.... .35

AE103, 7½x9½ inches.... **$0.18**
GE105, 8x14 inches....... .25
AE111, 10x15 inches...... .28

AA220, 7½x9½ inches.... **$0.18**
FA222, 8½x11½ inches... .20
AM109, 10x13½ inches.... .28

EL103, 7½x9½ inches.... **$0.15**
FL107, 8½x11½ inches... .20

OR1132, 8¼x12½ inches.. **$0.18**
ZR1133, 10x14 inches..... .22

OG156, 8½x12½ inches.. **$0.18**
ZK162, 10x13¾ inches.... .22
JG197, 13x18 inches...... .35

ZJ105, 8x14 inches....... **$0.22**
GD111, 10x15 inches...... .25

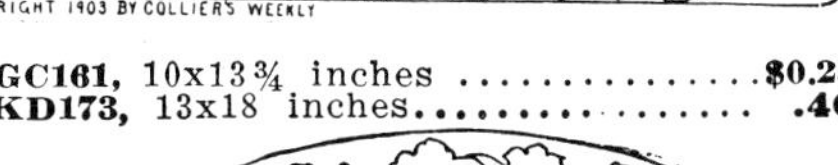

GC161, 10x13¾ inches **$0.25**
KD173, 13x18 inches................. .40

OH103, 7½x9½ inches.............. **$0.18**
H107, 8½x11½ inches .... .20
GH109, 10x13½ inches............ .25
JR114, 11½x15½ inches .... .35
MH117, 13½x16½ inches .... .50

FH155, 8½x12½ inches **$0.20**
JH167, 11¾x18 inches................ .35

JD113, 11½x15½ inches .... **$.35**
MD117, 13½x16½ inches .... .50
RD119, 14½x19½ inches .... .65

ZB192, 10x13¾ inches **$0.22**

OA188, 8½x12½ inches.............. **$0.18**

Three-Ply White Basswood Panels for Pyrographic Decoration

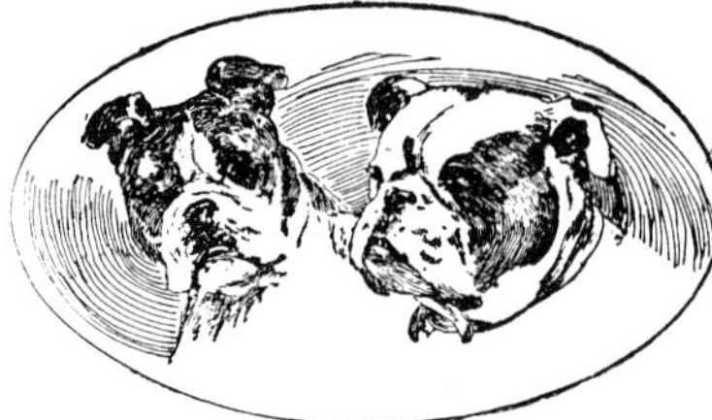

AP1110, 8x14 inches..............$0.22

AH105, 8x14 inches $0.22
GG111, 10x15 inches .... .25

AB180, 16x20 inches $0.48

GJ163, 10x14 inches......$0.25
LH176, 14x19 inches...... .45

EM154, 8x10 inches......$0.15
FM160, 10x12 inches..... .20

OU103, 7½x9½ inches....$0.18
FU107, 8½x11½ inches... .20
GC110, 10x13½ inches.... .25

FT1107, 8½x11½ inches..$0.20
GT1112, 10x13½ inches... .25

GB1127, 7x17 in......$0.25
KB1129, 9½x23 in... .40

OE188, 8½x12½ in.$0.18

OG155, 8½x12½ in....$0.18

OP1132, 8½x12½ in.$0.18
ZP1133, 10x14 in.... .22

GA1127, 7x17 in $ 0.25
KA1129, 9½x23 in .40

ZS192, 10x13¾ inches....$0.22
JS196, 13x18 inches...... .35

ZH161, 10x13¾ inches....$0.22
JH173, 13x18 inches...... .35

FD201, 8½x11½ inches...$0.20
GM218, 10x13½ inches... .25

AD201, 8½x11½ inches...$0.20
GD203, 10x13½ inches.... .25

Three-Ply Basswood Panels for Pyrographic Decoration

ED1202, 8 inches, **15c**   EA1202, 8 inches, **15c**   EG1202, 8 inches, **15c**   EE1202, 8 inches, **15c**   EH1202, 8 inches, **15c**

AM139, 16 inches $0.43
UM145, 22 inches.................... .80

FP1107, 8½x11½ inches $0.20
AP1115, 11½x15½ inches .... .33
PB119, 14½x19½ inches .... .60

JA137, 14 inches $0.35
AA141, 18 inches .... .48

FF133, 10 inches $0.20
JF137, 14 inches .... .35
PF143, 20 inches .... .60

AA180, 16x20 inches $0.48

FH133, 10 inches $0.20
JH137, 14 inches .... .35
PH143, 20 inches .... .65

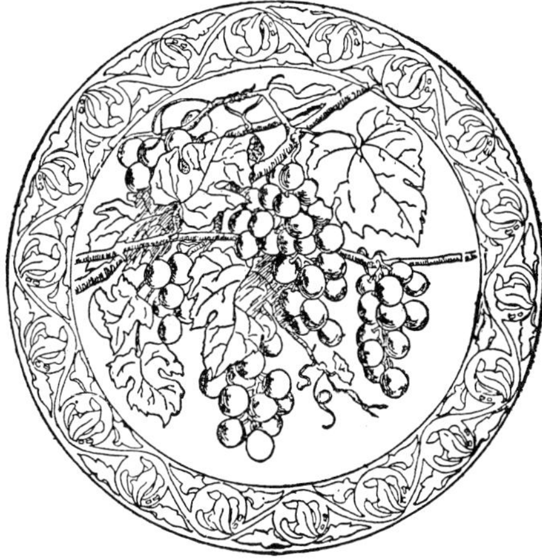

AG141, 18 inches $0.48

AK139, 16 inches $0.43
VK145, 22 inches .... .85

JP137, 14 inches $0.35
AD141, 18 inches .... .48

Naan Plush Cushion Covers for Pyrographic Decoration

All designs listed on this page are stamped on 18x18 inch Cushion Fronts.
Empire Green, Mahogany, Old Gold, Sea Green, Ecru.   Mention color desired when ordering.

PC842, 18x18 inches, front, **60c.**

PH826, 18x18 inches, front, **60c.**

PE826, 18x18 inches, front, **60c.**

PD842, 18x18 inches, front, **60c.**

PD826, 18x18 inches, front, **60c.**

PE842, 18x18 inches, front, **60c.**

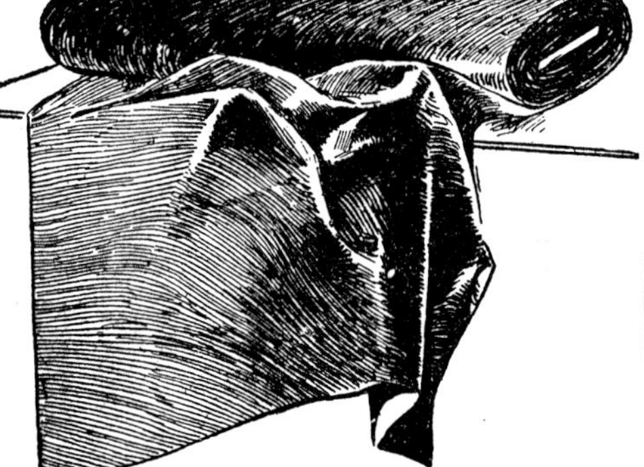

PJ819, 18x18 inches, front, **60c.**

Sofa Cushion Cords.
Furnished in shades to match Naan Plush.
3-yard piece heavy cord and two tassels; each...**$0.50**
Silk Ribbons.
For sofa cushion ruching, 3½ inches wide.
18x18 inches, liberal allowance for gathering;
each **$1.25**

PH820, 18x18 inches, front, **60c.**

Naan Plush is similar in appearance to
French Velour or Plush, but has several
very important features not to be found
in other goods of this nature. On other
makes of plushes excepting the Naan
the colors will spread beyond the outline
of the design, and the artistic results of
the work will be lost. Naan Plush is the
result of much study and experiment, and
we can recommend it as being superior
in every way to other fabrics. Samples
on application. Old Gold, Empire Green,
Sea Green, White. 52 inch, per yard.**$2.50**

**PLAIN BACKS FOR CUS-
HION COVERS.**

18x18, all colors, each, **45c.**

PU820, 18x18 inches, front, **60c.**